247 Property Tax Questions Answered

By

Arthur Weller

Publisher Details
This guide is published by Tax Portal Ltd. 3 Sanderson Close, Great Sankey, Warrington, Cheshire, WA5 3LN.

'247 Property Tax Questions Answered' – First published in June 2009. Second edition July 2010, Third edition May 2011. Fourth edition May 2012. Fifth edition April 2015. Sixth edition April 2016

Contents

About Arthur Weller

Arthur Weller is a tax specialist who advises other accountants. He is one of the most knowledgeable and respected tax specialists in the country. He is also the lead technical tax specialist and design consultant for www.property-tax-portal.co.uk.

Arthur is based in the northwest and qualified in 1997 as a certified accountant in a small firm of accountants. They specialised to a degree in property, and he worked for some years in their tax department.

He then moved on to a medium-sized firm, where he was the technical manager in the tax department.

In 1998 he passed the exams of the Institute of Taxation, and in June 2000 he left to set up his own tax consultancy.

Arthur works mainly in an advisory capacity for accountants in all areas of taxation. He also runs a telephone help line, giving phone advice on all areas of taxation to accountants around the country.

Much of his work has been focused in the following areas:

- property taxation (Arthur is regarded as a property tax specialist);
- capital gains tax;
- stamp duty;
- income tax;
- company tax.

Arthur also provides tax expertise to the following businesses:

Property Portfolio SOFTWARE	**Property Portfolio Software** UK's leading and triple award winning PC based property management software. Helps landlords to get better organised in every aspect of their property business. Visit: www.propertyportfoliosoftware.co.uk
landlord vision	**Landlord Vision** Landlord software solution that runs in the cloud. **Take your 30 day FREE Trial today.** Visit: www.landlordvision.co.uk

Tax Insider

A website providing monthly tax newsletters to help UK tax payers minimise their taxes.

Visit: www.taxinsider.co.uk

Income Tax

1. What Expenses Can I Offset Against Rental Income?

Question: I have just purchased my first buy-to-let property and have managed to successfully let it out. However I am unsure as to what expenses I can offset against my rental income.

Answer: Remember the golden rule: ***If you have incurred a revenue expense for the purpose of your property, then you can offset it against the rental income***.

This means that you can continue to lower your tax bill - *legitimately*. Most investors are aware that they can offset mortgage interest, insurance costs, rates, costs of decorating/repairs, wages and costs of services.

However, so many investors fail to claim the following costs, which when added together can provide a significant tax saving:

- Costs incurred when travelling back-and-to the investment property
- Advertisement costs
- Telephone calls made (or text messages sent) in connection with the property
- Cost of safety certificates
- Cost of bank charges (i.e. overdraft)
- Advisory fees e.g. legal and accountancy
- Subscription to property investment related magazines, products and services

2. Switch Property With Your Spouse

Question: My husband works full-time and I have the more difficult job of looking after the home and children, yet receive no income. Would it be better for me to own the property in my name?

Answer: If you have a spouse who is a lower rate (or even nil rate) taxpayer and you are a higher rate taxpayer, then consider moving the greater portion of the property ownership into their name. This means that a greater part of the profit will be attributed to the lower (or nil rate) taxpayer thus meaning that any tax liability could be significantly reduced.

This is a very powerful strategy if your spouse does not work, as any tax liability can be legitimately wiped out. Please note that in order to use this strategy you partner must be trustworthy as legally they will 'own' a greater share of the property.

3.   Any Tax Due For Unemployed Person?

Question: My wife owns our only buy-to-let property. There is no outstanding mortgage on the property and therefore it generates a monthly profit of £375. Is there any tax due on this profit, as she received no other income?

Answer: As you have mentioned that your wife receives no other income then there will be no tax due on the rental profits. This is because over the year she will make a profit of £4,500 (i.e. £375 * 12), and this amount is within the annual personal tax allowance, which for the 2016-2017 tax year is £11,000.

4.   I Am A Pensioner; Do I Still Need To Pay Tax?

Question: I am a pensioner and I have a property which I have rented to tenants for the past 15 years. Do I still have to pay tax on the property?

Answer: Yes, you do have to pay tax on the rental income from the property.

If it is your own house, rent-a-room relief may be applicable.

If the income is small, taking into account all your other taxable income, it may be covered by your age-related personal allowance, and, if applicable, married couple's allowance.

Therefore, after doing your sums, you may find that the rental income does not cause you to pay any or much taxation.

5.   Can I Change My 'Intention' To Help Reduce Tax?

Question: What would the tax treatment be if I were to buy a house with a view to doing it up and selling it for a profit, but then change my mind and decide that I would like to live there as my main residence.

In 1, 2 or 3 years' time when I sell the property, would I still have to pay tax as a developer or would I be allowed to claim PPR? I only ask this because the initial intent and the intent is one of the ways the IR use to determine which category you fall into.

Answer: ICTA 1988 sec 776 says that if a property is acquired with the intention of selling on at a profit, then that profit shall be subject to income tax, i.e. without the benefits of capital gains tax reliefs.

Paragraph 9 there says that this does not apply to a situation where it was the individual's private residence.

However, it refers you to TCGA 1992 sec 224 paragraph 3, where it says that if the acquisition was for the purpose of realising a gain, then principal private residence relief shall not apply.

This is not a clear cut matter. However, if there was a genuine change of mind it is quite possible that the Inspector would accept that the principal private residence relief should apply.

6.   The Most Tax Efficient Way To Take Out A Mortgage

Question: I own a property outright and want to rent it out once I've bought another, slightly bigger one. Tax-wise am I best taking out a mortgage on my original property and then using the cash as a deposit on my investment, or simply taking out the mortgage on the second property?

Answer: You are better off, tax wise, taking out the mortgage on your original property when you start to rent it out. This is because page BIM45700 on the Revenue manuals (Example 2) explains that in such circumstances the interest payable to the lender can be offset against the rental income, so that income tax is only paid on the net figure. (The tax writers explain that this applies when the amount of the loan is no greater than the market value of the house when it started to be rented out. If the loan exceeds this figure (e.g. in a case of re-mortgaging later on), the excess interest is not allowable.)

From April 2017 there are going to be new rules for a residential property landlord claiming relief for interest paid to a lender.

7. What Is Rent-A-Room Relief?

Question: I am thinking of letting out a single room in my home to a lodger. I have heard there is some sort of relief available for this. What is it and how do I claim it?

Answer: If you decide to let a room in your main residence, you can receive a rental income of up to £7,500 from 6th April 2016 and have no tax liability. In order to claim this allowance, the property must satisfy the following conditions:

- you must also live in the property
- the room you are letting out must be fully furnished

Prior to 6th April, the amount of relief that could be claimed was £4,250.

All that is necessary to claim this relief is to tick the rent-a-room box at the beginning of the land and property page of the tax return.

8. Can I Offset The Rent I Am Charged?

Question: My wife and I have lived in our property for 10 years. I am a member of HM Forces and in the summer we are posted away and have to live in Army married quarters. The rent for this is approx. £200pm. We will be renting our house out whilst I am posted. Can this £200 be offset against any income tax liability as I have no choice in the matter, and I did not plan to rent out my house to make profit, although it will produce a profit of £300pm?

Answer: The income of £500pm and the expense of £200pm are two separate items. The income is Schedule A rental income and should be declared in the Land and Property section of the Self-Assessment tax return. The expense of £200pm is an allowable expense and should be entered in box 17 on page 1 of the Employment section of the Self-Assessment return.

9. Can I Offset Property Losses Against Other Income?

Question: I have bought a property to let out and it is possible that in the first, and perhaps the second, year I will make a loss after accounting for insurances, mortgage interest and loan interest used to get a deposit. Can I offset that loss against my earnings from employment during the same period? If so which IR form do I need to use?

Answer: The answer is 'no'. The losses cannot be offset against your employment income. However, they can be carried forward and offset against future rental income profits that are generated from the property business.

If you have been making losses then it is important that you register those losses with the HMRC. The reason for this is because any losses can be carried forward and offset against future profits. For example, if in one tax year you made a £1,000 loss and then the following year you made a £1,000 profit, there is no tax liability as the £1,000 loss has been carried forward and wipes out your future gain!

However, if you have any other properties that are being rented out in the same tax year at a profit, then the loss from the loss-making property can be set off against the profit from the profit-making property.

10.   Is Property Now Classed As 'Business Income'?

Question: I'm told that property income is now deemed business income. Although it is investment income it is now deemed income for class 2 National insurance contributions.

I note that you do not mention this in your various replies because surely this should be advised to property investors as they would if the income exceeds the class 2 income limit be liable for a fine if they do not notify the authorities within 3 months of starting. You views would be appreciated.

Answer: Property letting will rarely be regarded as self-employment for NI purposes, although if the extent of the landlord's involvement in managing the lettings and looking after the properties is substantial (which might be particularly relevant for furnished holiday lettings), it is possible that the activities will constitute a business, in which case Class 2 NICs will be payable.

Class 4 NICs are only payable where income is taxed as trading income. Even though rents are now treated as being from a business in calculating property income, this is not the same as saying that a business actually exists, and it does not alter the NI position.

11.   Is There A Limit To The Amount That Can Be Claimed?

Question: Is there any limit to the amount you can borrow and still qualify for full tax relief on an interest only mortgage?

Answer: There is no limit providing all the borrowed funds are used 'wholly and exclusively' for the rental business. Where this is not the case, e.g. the taxpayer has a property that he is renting out and re-mortgages in order to withdraw capital from his business, to use for non-rental business purposes, then the amount of allowable interest is limited to the extent that the loan matches the value of the property when it first started to be used in the rental business.

Where the loan is greater, the interest on the excess is not allowable (unless as stated previously the funds are used for the rental business).

From April 2017 there are going to be new rules for a residential property landlord claiming relief for interest paid to a lender.

12.   Can I Offset The Cost Of Buying A Vehicle?

Question: Is it possible to offset the cost of buying a vehicle for use in your letting business, and if so, what would be the best way of doing this?

Answer: Here is a quote from the Revenue manuals page PIM2210:

Capital expenditure on providing the means to travel (usually a car or van) isn't deductible in computing rental business profits; nor is a depreciation charge. But plant and machinery capital allowances may be available. These allowances are deducted in computing the business profit or loss. The 'wholly and exclusively' rule applies to these allowances but, as with revenue expenditure, the landlord can claim the business proportion of the allowances. Plant and machinery allowances on cars costing more than £12,000 are also further restricted.

13.   Can Interest Be Claimed As A Business Expense?

Question: I have taken out an interest only mortgage on my PPR in order to finance my property development business and enable me to acquire property as a "cash buyer" prior to mortgaging on a Buy-to-let mortgage. Can this interest be claimed as a business expense?

Answer: If you have released equity out of your main home, i.e. increased the borrowing, and this additional money was used for buying further properties then the interest charged on the additional borrowing can be offset. This is because the additional loan has been used for the purpose of your property business and therefore the interest can be offset.

Consider the following case study:

> Ali is desperate to buy his first investment property after seeing his own house value almost double within 5 years. Due to his lavish lifestyle, he has no savings of his own but is in a well-paid job, earning £40,000 per annum.
>
> He sees an investment property advertised for £100,000, but his mortgage lender requests a deposit of £15,000. He sources this deposit by releasing an additional £15,000 of equity from his main home. The bank then agrees to finance the remaining £85,000.
>
> This means that Ali has a 100% financed investment property. It also means that he is able to offset the interest charged on both his equity release of £15,000 and the BTL £85,000 mortgage against his rental income.

14.   Can I Offset Money Paid To The Tenant?

Question: Having bought an investment property with a sitting tenant paying a low rent, I paid the tenant £20,000 to vacate and have now rented the property to a new tenant for 10 years at a much higher rent. Can I claim this premium as an expense against rental income or only as capital expenditure once the property is sold?

Answer: Firstly, from the High Court case Wateys London Ltd. v Pike (1982) quoted by the HMRC's Business Income Manual page BIM35545, it can be seen that this is capital expenditure, not revenue.

Secondly, in order to be allowable expenditure to offset against the sale proceeds when the property is sold, as enhancement expenditure under TCGA 1992 sec 38 paragraph

1(b), it must reflected in the state or nature of the asset at the date of disposal (HMRC Capital Gains Tax Manual page CG15180).

Page CG71262 there says that if, after obtaining vacant possession, the landlord granted a new lease on essentially the same terms, the benefit would not be there at the date of disposal, and therefore the expenditure would not be allowable.

However, in this case, the new rent is much higher, so, by implication, this payment to the old tenant should be an allowable capital expenditure when the property is sold.

15.   Should I Contact HMRC Myself?

Question: I have had a BTL property for nearly 2 years. I am in PAYE employment so rarely get a tax return to complete. Can I wait till I get a tax return to complete before declaring it or would that be counterproductive?

Answer: If a taxpayer receives any taxable income in a tax year of which the HMRC is unaware, then they have a legal duty to inform the HMRC about this by 5 October.

So, for example, if any income was received between 6 April 2014 and 5 April 2015, then the individual must inform HMRC by 5 October 2015.

16.   Can I Offset These Losses?

Question: In year one, I earned income from a house sale, but made a loss from a house sale in year two. Can I offset the loss incurred in year two against income earned in year one, or alternatively any income that is earned in year three?

Answer: The answer to this question depends on whether we are discussing capital gains and losses, or trading gains and losses.

If the two houses sold are investment assets, so that in year 1 you made a capital gain and in year 2 you made a capital loss, then the general rule is that a capital loss cannot be carried back and offset against a capital gain in a previous year (see CG15811). However the capital loss in year 2 can be carried forward to set off against a capital gain in year 3, or future years (see CG15810).

However if you are a property developer so that in year 1 you made a trading gain, and in year 2 you made a trading loss, then the story is different. A trading loss in a tax year can be set off against general income of the tax year of loss and/or the previous tax year. BIM85015. Alternatively, this trading loss can be carried forward to a future tax year to be set off against profits of the same trade (see BIM85060).

17.   Is There A Difference When Offsetting Interest?

Question: When offsetting mortgage interest payments, does it matter if the mortgage is 'interest only' or a 'repayment mortgage'?

Answer: No, it does not matter. The interest charged on both mortgages can be offset against the rental income. What this means in reality is that if you have an 'interest only' mortgage then the **full** mortgage payment will be offset.

However, if you have a 'Repayment' mortgage then only the 'interest repayment' part of the mortgage will be offset. You will not be able to offset the capital part of the repayment. This means that you need to find out from your bank for each payment what part was 'interest' and what part was 'capital'. In most cases you find this out when the mortgage lender sends you your end of year complete mortgage statement.

From April 2017 there are going to be new rules for a residential property landlord claiming relief for interest paid to a lender.

18.   Can I Lease My Commercial Property To My Company?

Question: I recently read about the tax benefits of purchasing a commercial property in my own name, then leasing it to my Ltd Company which then rents it out to a sole trader or unlisted company at a slightly higher rent.

I have owned a commercial property for over 12 years and leased it out to 2 different retailers. Is it possible to put this new found knowledge into plan and get the leaseholders to pay their rent to my property investment Ltd Co. instead of me, then for me to invoice the company for the rent minus say 10%?

Answer: Yes, it is possible to start putting this plan into action now but the legal agreements must be properly drawn up. You don't need to limit yourself to 10%. You can make the margin greater than this.

19.   Can My Client Re-Arrange His Affairs To Offset Interest?

Question: Can interest relief can be claimed in the following scenario:-

The client
a) owns a PPR valued at £900k with a mortgage secured on it of £400k
b) subsequently acquires a buy-to let property purchased for £450k with a mortgage of £200k secured, using savings to fund the deposit without actually re-mortgaging or physically transferring money.

Is the client allowed to 're-arrange his affairs' by deeming that £60,000 of the existing mortgage secured on the PPR is funding/replacing the deposit on the letting property, and hence claim a tax deduction in his Schedule 'A' comp for the interest on the £60,000?

Answer: The interest is not allowable. The loan was originally taken out for the purpose of purchasing the PPR, and it is not possible to "re-arrange matters". The taxpayer would have to physically transfer money or actually re-mortgage.

20.   When Do I Pay My Tax If I Have Sold A Property?

Question: I have sold a property in June 2015. When do I need to declare the sale to the HMRC and when do I need to pay the tax by?

Answer: Your property has been sold in the 2015-2016 tax year which started on April 6th 2015 and ends on April 5th 2016. This means that you need to notify the HMRC of your sale in the 2015-2016 tax return.

If you complete a paper return, then you must return your completed paper form by 31 October 2016. You will then be required to pay any tax due by 31st January 2017.

Alternatively, if you file online, then the tax return must be completed and returned with any tax due by 31st January 2017.

21.   Can We Merge Our Portfolio And Split The Income?

Question: My Partner (life) and I operate 3 BTL's. She owns 1 and we jointly own 2. When completing tax-returns can we merge all 3 and split 50/50?

Answer: If the first property is solely in her name and not in joint ownership, it cannot be merged with the other two properties and must be attributed only to her. The remaining two properties, assuming they are 50-50 owned, can be split 50-50 for income tax purposes.

22.   How Do I Handle General Portfolio Costs?

Question: I have a number of properties but some costs are generic and cannot be attributed to a single property. Is it possible to offset a cost against a single property or do I need to apportion them? For example, I purchased some decoration materials for painting and decorating two of my properties. Can I just offset the cost against one property?

Answer: In any tax year, all income and expenses from all the properties owned and rented out by a landlord operating a Schedule A property rental business are amalgamated and combined into one single account – for tax purposes. So the answer to your question is that as long as the cost is attributed to the correct tax year in which it occurred, it doesn't make a difference which property it was for.

23.   Can I Bring My Undeclared Loss Forward?

Question: Last tax year I made a loss on my property rental business but did not declare this to the HMRC. I now understand that I can bring this loss forward to the current year in which I have made a profit, and offset it against my property profits. Is this true?

Answer: Yes, it's possible to bring forward any rental income losses and offset them against any gains made in the current year. This is a very good practice, which unfortunately too many investors are unaware of.

24.   I Rent Storage. Can I Offset The Costs?

Question: I have some flats on rental. Sometimes I have to remove furniture from a flat because the tenant does not like a particular piece. I therefore rent storage space in which

I keep a supply of items of furniture which move into and out of any one of up to 7 flats. Can the rental charges be placed against my income in the same way as other (allowable) expenses?

Answer: Yes, the cost of renting storage space is allowable. The reason is that it fulfils the principal criteria of "wholly and exclusively", as the cost was incurred for the purpose of your property business. If you had never rented property, then you would not be incurring such costs.

Case Study:

John owns 5 properties which are all fully furnished. However, he finds a new long-term tenant for his property who has his own furniture and furnishings. John decides that he will empty the property and store the furniture in rented storage. The cost of rental storage is £450. This amount can be offset against the rental income as it has been incurred 'wholly and exclusively' for the purpose of the rental business.

25.   Look To Claim Costs As 'Revenue Costs'?

Question: I have been advised to always try to claim costs as 'Revenue Costs' wherever possible. Why should I do this?

Answer: The simple reason is that it improves your cash flow and means that you do not have to wait until you dispose of the property before you can claim the expense. By claiming it is a 'Revenue Cost' you can offset it against your annual rental income, which means that ultimately you could be paying little or no income tax.

26.   I Am Unsure If The Cost Is A Capital Cost

Question: I am having my single glazing windows replaced with double glazing windows. Can I offset the cost as a 'Revenue Cost' or a 'Capital Cost'?

Answer: Sometimes it is easy to determine whether a cost is of a capital nature or not. For example, if you have had a new conservatory built or even a new bedroom added, then this is clearly a capital expense. This is because it has increased the value of the property. However, sometimes distinguishing between the two costs is not so clear.

Consider the replacement of windows. If you currently have rotten single glazed windows, you will be able to replace them with UPVC double glazed windows and offset the entire cost against the rental income. There will be no need to class this as a 'capital cost'.

This is because it is generally accepted that the standard windows used in modern properties are UPVC and not wooden single glazed windows. So you are replacing the current standard window fitting with a like-for-like window.

Remember: if you can class a cost as a 'revenue' cost then it will improve your cash-flow as you will pay less property income tax.

27. Can I Claim My Costs For Re-Mortgaging?

Question: I have heard that mortgage broker and mortgage lender fees are of a revenue nature and valuation costs are of a capital nature. Is this also true if an investment property is re-mortgaged? I am about to re-mortgage an investment property with a different lender and will incur these costs again, but am unsure if I can claim relief against them.

Answer: The answer is that it depends on the status of the interest on the loan. If the interest on the loan is an allowable expense, the cost of obtaining the loan is also an allowable expense. So in this particular instance, because the loan that is being re-mortgaged is for the purpose of the property then once again the costs can be offset. (See the Revenue manuals page PIM2015 paragraph 7.)

Again, the mortgage broker and mortgage lender fees will be claimed against your rental income, and the valuation costs will be claimed once you decide to sell the property.

Case Study:

> John has a buy-to-let mortgage with an outstanding amount of £50,000. He is currently repaying £450 per calendar month back to the bank. However, he realizes that another lender has a special reduced interest rate, so if he re-mortgages with them his monthly rate will be reduced to £400.
>
> He re-mortgages the property and incurs costs as follows:
>
> - Mortgage broker fees £250

- Mortgage lender fees £200
- Survey costs £200

This means he can offset £450 against his annual rental income and can claim the survey costs when he decides to sell the property.

28. Are These Costs Of A 'Capital' Or 'Revenue' Nature?

Question: Could you please clarify whether the following costs are deemed to be 'capital' or 'revenue'.

a) Mortgage broker fees i.e. I have paid a mortgage broker a % arrangement fee

b) Mortgage lenders arrangement fee

c) Property valuation costs

Answer: The Property Income Manual page PIM2066 says: "Costs you incur in obtaining loan finance for your rental business are generally deductible in computing rental business profits provided they relate wholly and exclusively to property let out on a commercial basis.

These costs include loan fees, commissions, guarantee fees and fees in connection with the security of a loan."

This means that a) and b) are classed as revenue expenditures and can therefore be offset against the rental income.

Property valuation costs are dependent on the purpose for which the valuation was obtained. If for the purpose of buying or selling the property, then they will be capital costs. If for insurance purposes, then they will be revenue expenses. See the Revenue manuals page PIM2205.

So, to summarize, a) and b) are Revenue Costs and can be offset against your annual rental income and c) is a dependent on the purpose for which the valuation was obtained.

29.   Do I Need To Have Receipts?

Question: Do you have to have receipts in order to claim property related expenditures? What happens if you do not have a receipt or have lost them?

Answer: If you know in your heart that you did spend the money on an allowable expense, then you can claim it. However, if the HMRC question you about it and you cannot prove it, then you must be prepared for the HMRC to say to you: 'We don't believe you and therefore we are not accepting what you say'.

Thus, although you are allowed to claim it because you know it is true, you must be prepared to pay the tax on it if questioned about it whilst being unable to prove it.

30.   Re-Mortgaging A Property After Cash Purchase

Question: There is one issue I've not been able to get a clear answer to. I consulted a few accountants on this and still did not get a satisfactory answer.

If I purchase a property with cash and then get a mortgage on it in the next few months, can I still offset the interest on that mortgage against the tax?

Answer: In my opinion, the mortgage interest is allowable in this particular scenario. This is because the property was bought with the **intention** to take out the mortgage soon afterwards. In this scenario it appears as though the purchaser only paid cash originally because this was a better way to execute the purchase. For example, sometimes investors need to move quickly and applying for a mortgage can take several weeks.

Because it was always the intention to fund the property business by means of the mortgage, it will be possible to offset the interest.

Case Study:

> John has inherited £100,000 from his father's estate.
>
> He is presented with the opportunity to purchase a property at £100,000, but he must complete within two weeks. By purchasing within two weeks, he will save £25,000 off the original asking price of £125,000.

John knows that it will take too long to apply for a buy-to-let mortgage, so he pays for the property with cash.

Two months later he re-mortgages the property using a standard buy-to-let mortgage.

In this scenario John can offset the interest on the re-mortgage, as it was always his intention to fund the investment by a mortgage.

31.   Offsetting The Cost Of A £5,000 Property Seminar

Question: I have just attended a £5,000 property investment training course. Can I offset this entire cost against my future property rental income?

Answer: The short answer to your question is this: if it is wholly and exclusively for the purposes of the trade presently carried on by the taxpayer, then it is allowable.

Here is what the HMRC has to say about the matter:

'Expenditure on training courses attended by the proprietor of a business with the purpose of up-dating his or her skills and professional expertise is normally revenue expenditure, which is deductible from profits of the business provided it is incurred wholly and exclusively for the purposes of the trade or profession carried on by the individual at the time the training is undertaken'.

So what does that mean? Well, if you are already a property investor with a portfolio and attend the course to update your investment skills, you **can** offset the entire cost as you will be regarded as updating your skills.

However, if you want to start investing in property and attend a course to learn how to do this, then you will not be able to offset the costs against the rental income. You **cannot** offset the cost as you will not be 'updating' your skills in your current profession as you are effectively learning a new profession.

A word of warning - If you do decide to make a claim, it could well trigger an investigation.

This is because the HMRC does keep a close eye on large amounts being claimed, so be warned!

32.   Can I Claim Tax Relief On Drawdown Money?

Question: I am planning to take a drawdown on two of my properties and hold the money for a short time until I find another property to buy. As I intend reinvesting the drawdown money as a deposit on another property can I claim tax relief on all the interest paid on the new mortgages of the original properties.

Answer: If it is clear that the money was borrowed in order to purchase the new property, then all the interest on the new loan is allowable. The HMRC may challenge the taxpayer, and ask them to prove that the purpose of the loan was for the requirements of their property business.

If the taxpayer can show that the loan was taken out only a short time before being reinvested, and the taxpayer did not use the money for any other purpose during the time between borrowing and reinvesting, they should be OK.

Even if the intervening time period is not so short, but the taxpayer can show that they were actively looking for another property to invest in, and they needed the money immediately available just in case the opportunity for a cash purchase came their way, this would also be a reasonable argument.

33.   Can I Maximise Tax Relief?

Question: I have a portfolio of 8 properties bought over a number of years with individual repayment mortgages outstanding against them. I would like to know if it is possible to maximise the tax relief available by grouping the value of the portfolio together and offsetting the total value of loan interest or do I have to re finance each property and mortgage individually to maximise the interest relief.

Answer: In most cases all the various types of income from land and property in the UK are treated as parts of the same, single rental business. It does not matter how many properties the taxpayer has, or how many different types of income from land and property. This means that normally all the rental business receipts and expenditure can be lumped together and, hence, that the expenses on one property can be deducted from the receipts of another, (ICTA88/S21 (4)).

34.   Can Service Charges Be Deducted?

Question: Can all service charges and building Improvements carried out by a Leasehold Management Company be deducted as a cost from the rental income of a Buy-to-Let property?

Answer: All service charges can be deducted. Building improvements can be deducted if they are revenue expenses but not if they are capital expenses. It is not easy to distinguish between the two but, in a nutshell, revenue expenses are small repairs and general upkeep, like painting and 'like for like' replacements, whereas capital expenses are extensions, big repairs and replacements that are a major upgrade from the original.

35.   Can I Transfer The Property?

Question: I am currently looking into transferring a rental property into my wife's name in order to take advantage of her personal tax allowance, half of which she is not using. This could mean the majority of our rental income (about £4,000 a year) would be tax free.

I understand that I do not have to transfer any legal ownership to my wife, but I will need a declaration of trust. Can I transfer 100 per cent of the property income to my wife and, if so, will all paperwork (bills etc.) relating to the property need to be in my wife's name?

I have made an appointment to see a tax adviser as I am aware that I need to do this properly, and, like most tax matters, it is a little more complicated than I originally thought.

Answer: What you have written is correct. The beneficial ownership needs to be transferred to your wife, and this can be done by a declaration of trust. If you transfer 100% of the property to your wife then you will succeed in transferring 100% of the property income to her. All the paperwork relating to the property should be in your wife's name.

36. Can My Son Live Rent Free In UK Property?

Question: I am an Irish national living outside of the EU. I am purchasing a property in the UK in a non-resident company. I propose to allow my son, who lives in the UK, to live in the property rent free - is there any reason why I cannot do this?

Answer: If the son is neither a shareholder nor an employee (e.g. director) of the company, and only the parent is a shareholder and / or employee of the company, then there is no reason why you cannot do this.

The parent is not UK resident, so not liable to UK tax.

The son is UK resident and receiving a gift, but since he is not a shareholder, it cannot be deemed a distribution from the company; and since he not an employee of, nor does any work for, the company, it cannot be deemed a benefit in kind being received by virtue of his employment.

(There was a court case (Newfields Development) the outcome of which said that HMRC can attribute any shares held by associates to an individual, irrespective of whether that individual is a shareholder in the company - but I don't think that it is relevant in this case.)

37. Can Our Property Business Hire My Self-Employed Partner

Question: My partner and I are developing a large property into three flats. My partner is a self-employed plumber and is carrying out most of the work himself. Is it acceptable for his plumbing firm to invoice our development partnership for work carried out at the property?

Answer: Yes, it is acceptable for his plumbing firm to invoice your development partnership for work carried out at the property. I assume that he will charge standard commercial rates, in the same way that he would do work for anyone else, and not charge more. Since he is declaring the income earned from this work, and paying tax on it, it makes no difference to HMRC that your partner does the work or any other professional plumber.

38.   Is My Building Of A House Classed As A Property Trade?

Question: If I bought land and built and house and subsequently sold it, am I still liable for capital gains tax or will I be treated like a property trader who pays no capital gains?

Answer: You will be treated like a property trader who pays no capital gains tax, but instead pays income tax on their profits. If I understand correctly, you sold the property soon after it was completed and did not rent it out.

This may even have been your intention when you started. If so, the Revenue will argue that this is not an investment, which is subject to capital gains tax when sold, but that you are a trader selling a commodity, and so subject to income tax.

39.   Will My Rental Income Affect My Tax Credits?

Question: Will rental income affect my tax credit, if the mortgage interest cost is just equal to the rental income?

Answer: If the mortgage interest, which is an allowable expense, costs just equal to the rental income, then your **net rental income** is nil, and your tax credit will not be affected.

Income, for tax credit purposes, is calculated in much the same way as for income tax.

Only net rental income (income that remains after deducting allowable expenses) counts, not gross rental income (income before deduction of allowable expenses).

From April 2017 there are going to be new rules for a residential property landlord claiming relief for interest paid to a lender.

40.   Non-Refundable Fees – How Will I Be Taxed?

Question: I sell houses on a Rent-to-Own basis using option agreements. How will I be taxed on the non-refundable, up front option fee as I will not know if they are buying for the next three years? Also, what happens if they buy/don't buy as this money comes off the purchase price?

Answer: To answer your question, here is a quote from the Revenue Capital Gains Manual page CG12350:

In consideration of a payment by A to B of £100, B grants to A an option to buy a chargeable asset from him within 3 months for £15,000. If B did not incur any allowable expenditure he has a chargeable gain of £100 from the disposal of the option. This is assessable for the year in which the option was granted.

If A abandons the option there is no loss relief to him and B remains liable on a chargeable gain of £100. If A exercises the option his cost of acquisition is £15,000 + £100 = £15,100 and the same figure is used in calculating B's chargeable gain for the year in which the option is exercised.

If B has already been assessed on the £100 gain from the disposal of the option itself that assessment should be discharged, or reduced if other gains are included in the assessment and if the tax has been paid it should be set off against the tax payable on the gain on the disposal of the asset.

If you have always had beneficial ownership over half the property, then the proposed sale from your brother to you can only be for his half of the property, because you already own your half.

Any sale between connected persons (and brothers are called connected persons) is treated for capital gains tax purposes, as a sale at present market value, regardless of the actual payment the buyer makes to the seller.

So in your case, even if you pay your brother £100,000, and no more, the Revenue will treat your brother as though he received £150,000 (the current market value) from you, for capital gains tax purposes, and tax him accordingly.

41.   Starting Out As A Landlord?

Question: I am starting out as a landlord with my first property and I don't know how I need to report my taxes. How do I sort these out and who could I talk to, to find out?

Answer: Keep a record of all your rental income and allowable expenses (attributable to your rental business) from 6 April until the following 5 April. Then amalgamate all the income and expenditure and draw up an income and expenditure account for that period.

42.   Can I Claim Mortgage Relief?

Question: I unsuccessfully tried to sell a rental property over a period of 9 months (various buyers dropped out for various reasons!). The property was untenanted (i.e. vacant possession for sale) after the first 2 months of the 9 month period but is now rented again.

Can I claim mortgage interest relief for the period in which I was trying to sell the property but had not instructed the letting agent to market the property.

Answer: On page PIM2105 of the Revenue Property Income Manual the Revenue say:

"A property may be let for short periods in a tax year or only part of it may be let throughout a tax year (or both); the rest of the time the property is used for private or non-business purposes. Here the interest charged on a qualifying loan on that property has to be split between the rental business use and the private or non-business use.

The split is done in whatever way produces a fair and reasonable business deduction, taking account of both the proportion of business use and the length of business use.

You don't have to split the interest if the taxpayer is genuinely trying to let the property but it is empty because they have not been able to find a tenant. In this case the interest will meet the 'wholly and exclusively' test.

It won't meet this test if they have not been trying to let the property or they have been using it for private or non-business purposes."

It would appear from this that if in a period you were not trying to let the property then for that period of time you cannot claim mortgage interest relief.

43.   Are We Liable To Tax On Interest Free Loans?

Question: If we give our two sons an interest free loan to buy a 50% share in our property (which they are also living in) would we be liable to tax on the monthly repayments from them (£700 per month)?

We would have this drawn up legally with an agreed value and fixed loan period.

Answer: If the loan is interest free, they are only paying back capital and you are not earning anything from the loan. So there can be no tax on the monthly repayments from them.

44.   Can I Offset The Repayments?

Question: Back in 2004 I took my company pension at the early age of 50 years.

My reason for doing this was that my income at the time was low and I believed that the state of the company might have led to the pension's demise. Over the last 6 years my situation has improved to the point that I now pay 40% tax on all my earnings. Is there any way I can defer or put my pension that I took early into a scheme that will not be taxed at source?

Answer: Your question is not really a tax question but has to do with pension scheme rules. You really need to ask your pension provider about the feasibility of deferring the receipt of your annuity until a year in which your income drops below the higher rate tax threshold, even though you have begun to take it.

Have you taken the 25% tax free lump sum? Speak to your pension provider about crystallisation and the possibility of not drawing the income to which you are entitled.

45.   Can I Pay A Family Member To Manage My Property?

Question: I have a property in my hometown and live elsewhere. It is currently for sale but being rented whilst trying to sell.

Rather than pay a mortgage company to be on call, can I pay any other family member a nominal monthly fee to be on call for any problems, emergencies, etc. so long as it is similar or less in price than an agency would charge for an equivalent service?

Answer: You can pay a family member to do the job you would have asked an agency to do, and pay them the normal price for the job as long as it is equivalent to a normal commercial arrangement. Make sure regular payments are made from your bank account into a bank account in their name and that the amounts you pay them are reasonable. And that they actually do the job!

46.   Can We Offset Our Cost?

Question: My wife & I own a flat that we use occasionally at weekends when we visit our hometown in Liverpool. We live in rented accommodation in the south of England due to current work commitments. We plan to rent the flat out on a short term basis (per night) that will allow us to still have occasional use, and in this tax year we would expect to get around +/- 90 nights of rent.

Can we offset the costs i.e. mortgage, council tax and service charges of the flat for the full tax year against income tax on this rent?

We understand that any use of the flat by ourselves would be deducted from any tax relief.

Answer: Here is a quote from the Revenue Property Income Manual page PIM2105 about interest payments but the same applies to mortgage, council tax and service charges:

"A property may be let for short periods in a tax year or only part of it may be let throughout a tax year (or both); the rest of the time the property is used for private or non-business purposes. Here the interest charged on a qualifying loan on that property has to be split between the rental business use and the private or non-business use. The split is done in whatever way produces a fair and reasonable business deduction, taking account of both the proportion of business use and the length of business use.

You don't have to split the interest if the taxpayer is genuinely trying to let the property but it is empty because they have not been able to find a tenant. In this case the interest will meet the 'wholly and exclusively' test. It won't meet this test if they have not been trying to let the property or they have been using it for private or non-business purposes."

47.   Is This A Good Idea...?

Question: My partner and I are unmarried. We are buying a principal private residence in joint names (with a mortgage) as well as an investment property (with no mortgage) which will be let out to students.

My partner is a higher tax rate earner whereas I am a lower tax rate earner and irregularly employed.

We wish to limit the amount of income tax payable on the rental income and eventual capital gains on the let property when we sell it. I know there are various scenarios we can employ here.

Currently we are thinking of owning the rental property (99% to me, the lower tax earner, and 1% to my partner, to limit the income tax we have to pay. Then when the time comes to sell we plan to get married and share the second house 50% each without paying tax on the transfer.

This will allow us to both use our full CG exemption for the year. Furthermore, we are thinking of living in the second property as our primary residence for several months before we sell it.

Is this a good idea, or am I way off the mark?

Answer: It is not necessary to split the ownership of the investment property 99:1. On page PIM1030 of the Revenue Property Income Manual it is explained that two people (who are not spouses) can make an agreement that the property income is received in a different proportion to their underlying ownership. So you can buy the property 50:50, but make a written agreement between you about the receipt of rental income before you start renting out.

Re: living in the property, it is a good idea if you can show that you move in with the intention to live there long term, and you actually live there for an extended period - I would say six months to a year at least. During that period you will lose the principal private residence status for the first house that you have occupied until then as your main residence, because one cannot have two main residences (for tax purposes) concurrently.

48.   Can I Deduct Capital Expenses From Profits?

Question: Tax law states that you can deduct from the profit you have from the sale of a rental property anything you have done to enhance its value (but not repairs and maintenance). HM Revenue & Customs (HMRC) gives the example of an extension. My question is: can I deduct the cost of installing central heating, a new bathroom and a new kitchen?

Answer: In one sentence, the answer to your question is that you can claim the cost of installing central heating, a new bathroom and a new kitchen if a) you did not previously claim these costs as revenue expenditure against your rental income, and b) the new installations were a considerable improvement over the corresponding heating, bathroom and kitchen that were in the property before.

Here is a quote from the HMRC Property Income Manual page PIM2020, talking about claiming the cost of installing a new kitchen as a repair, against rental income:

'For example, if a fitted kitchen is refurbished the type of work carried out might include the stripping out and replacement of base units, wall units, sink etc., re-tiling, work top replacement, repairs to floor coverings and associated re-plastering and re-wiring. Provided the kitchen is replaced with a similar standard kitchen then this is a repair and the expenditure is allowable.

If at the same time additional cabinets are fitted, increasing the storage space, or extra equipment is installed, then this element is a capital addition and not allowable (applying whatever apportionment basis is reasonable on the facts).

But if the whole kitchen is substantially upgraded, for example if standard units are replaced by expensive customised items using high quality materials, the whole expenditure will be capital.'

49.   Can I Claim VAT on Purchased Property?

Question: If I buy a property as a new company and carry out building work (new and repair), can I claim back the VAT spent. Can I also then pay myself with dividends?

Generally, if the property is a residential property then a landlord is making exempt supplies and whether he is an individual or a company, he cannot reclaim back the VAT spent on new building works and repairs on an existing property. However, VAT is charged at the reduced rate of 5% on the supply of services and building materials for the conversion of non-residential property into dwellings, conversion of residential property into a different number of dwellings, conversion of residential or non-residential property into a multiple occupancy dwelling and the bringing into use of a property that has been empty for three years and some other circumstances.

You can always pay yourself dividends from your company, provided the company has enough distributable profits in the profit and loss account to do so.

See pages CTM20090/5 on the HMRC manuals:

http://www.hmrc.gov.uk/manuals/ctmanual/ctm20090.htm

http://www.hmrc.gov.uk/manuals/ctmanual/ctm20095.htm

50.   Can I Offset Interest from Our Re-Mortgage?

Question: We wish to raise about £45,000 on two properties that we originally paid cash for 10 years ago, purchase price jointly at £45,000. The money is to be used for the balance on a holiday cottage. Can I offset the interest only portion of this mortgage against our other investment property income if we use the holiday cottage for private use only or must we encompass the cottage into our portfolio as a holiday letting?

Answer: Since the amount of the £45,000 mortgage does not exceed the amount you paid for the house originally, you are entitled to offset all the interest on the £45,000 mortgage against your gross rental income from all your rental properties. I am assuming that these two properties that originally cost you £45,000 cash are part of your present rental portfolio, i.e. that you actually rent them out.

Consequently you can use the £45,000 for private purposes and therefore the holiday cottage does not need to be rented out but can be used only privately if you so wish. See page BIM45700, http://www.hmrc.gov.uk/manuals/bimmanual/bim45700.htm, (example 2) on HMRC Business Income Manual.

From April 2017 there are going to be new rules for a residential property landlord claiming relief for interest paid to a lender.

51.   Should I Buy in Sole or Joint Name?

Question: I am trying to work out what my options are if I/we buy a property to do up and sell on using the equity from our main residence. The question is whether to buy in just my name or in joint names with my husband and, in this particular case, would income be subject to CGT or income tax if we did manage to sell?

If we do not manage to sell, my contingency plan would be to rent the property out for a period of time. I am currently not working though if this project succeeds, I might consider future developments. My husband and I currently rent out a property which was our main residence many years ago, and is jointly owned and my husband is a 40% taxpayer.

Answer: If you buy a property, do it up and sell on, the profits would be subject to income tax, because this is a trading venture. If you rent out the property, you will be in receipt of rental income, which again is subject to income tax.

In light of the fact that you currently do not work, which I presume means that you have little or no income, but your husband is a 40% taxpayer, it would seem the best option for you to buy only in your name so that any profits will be subject to your marginal rate of income tax i.e. 20% and not your husband's rate of 40%.

However, you need to consider the effect of buying in your own name, and not in joint names, on the possibility of getting a loan to do the project and the rate of interest you pay your lender, and, if you decide to take out a joint loan, whether you can offset all of the interest against your personal business venture.

52.   Can I Pay Myself for the Time Spent on Managing My Property Business?

Question: I live and run my UK properties from Cyprus. I find that I am spending a lot of time keeping my portfolio up to date, for which I am not being paid. If I was a tax resident of the UK, regardless of whether I paid myself for looking after the rental properties or not, I would still need to declare my worldwide income and be taxed accordingly. This is a 'catch 22' situation but as I am a tax resident of Cyprus, I only need to declare my UK income to the UK tax authorities. Therefore, if I pay myself in Cyprus for the work I carry out here with regards to my UK properties, can I then claim this on my tax returns? Obviously I would then have to declare this to my own tax authority and be taxed accordingly but the tax relief bracket is higher here so less tax would have to be paid.

Answer: On page PIM2080 of HMRC's Property Income Manual (http://www.hmrc.gov.uk/manuals/pimmanual/pim2080.htm), it states:

"A landlord can't deduct anything for the time they spend themselves working in their own rental business."

So even though you put time and effort into your property business, you cannot put a monetary value on that time and effort and claim it as an allowable business expense, under UK property tax rules.

53. Should I Pay Cash Or Get a Mortgage to Purchase Buy to Let Property?

Question: I have a quick question regarding the deduction of mortgage interest from tax on the rental income generated from a buy to let. Basically, I was wondering, if I bought a property in cash and then got a mortgage on it almost immediately, would this be acceptable for tax deduction (as opposed to buying it with a mortgage in place)?

The reason being twofold: firstly, I think that the mortgage lender is keener for me to do this, and secondly, I am afraid I will lose out on the property if I don't move quickly.

I want the other cash to purchase another property. I am in the somewhat luxurious position of being cash rich but with no income. This makes mortgages somewhat of a problem, despite the fact that I have the cash to buy outright with plenty to spare. The point of the exercise would be to give me an income (the rent covers the mortgage interest and plenty spare).

Answer: In short, I believe that the interest payments are allowable, one reason being because you use cash in order to be able to purchase the property quickly, and if you do not use cash you possibly may not be able to make the purchase, and your intention all along is to substitute a mortgage soon afterwards, and the cash is merely in place of a bridging loan.

54.   Are These Legitimate Expenses?

Question: We purchased four buy to let properties during 09-10. Each one needed decorating and re carpeting prior to letting to make them clean and habitable. We had one boiler condemned and replaced and had to make electrics safe prior to occupation. Are these legitimate expenses to set against our tax liability for 2009-10?

Answer: If you look on the HMRC website on the Property Income Manual pages PIM2020 & PIM2505:

http://www.hmrc.gov.uk/manuals/pimmanual/PIM2020.htm
http://www.hmrc.gov.uk/manuals/pimmanual/PIM2505.htm

You will see that if the property was in a fit state to rent out when you purchased it and the purchase price was not significantly reduced due to the property being in a bad state, then any standard 'repairs and renewals' that would be allowable against rental income in the middle of tenancy are similarly allowable before the first tenancy begins.

55.   How Do I Go About Submitting a Tax Return Without the Help of an Accountant?

Question: I hold Power of Attorney (POA) for my Mother who is in a home and pays all her own costs. Her house is rented out to meet some of these, since February 2010. The house was empty for 2 months this autumn. I need to notify the Tax office but I plan to do the return myself to try and save money. Could you please give me some idea how to go about this?

Answer: You need to complete the UK property supplementary pages of the self-assessment tax return. I would advise you to look at the UK property notes that accompany the form. For the 2015 tax year the links are UK property (2015) and UK property notes (2015) respectively.

56.   How Long Should I Live In A Property For It To Become My Main Residence?

Question: My partner, who has lived with me for the last two years, has a property that he lived in for 3 years, before moving in with me. He is letting out his property but at some point we will want to buy together and sell both properties. My understanding was that you only needed to live in a property you have let out for 6 months at some point to not be taxed, but are you saying there is some rule regarding letting it for more or less than 3 years or living in it for more or less than 3 years?

My situation is that I have had four buy to let properties for a few years now. I will sell them off one by one eventually. The only way I can avoid tax is by living in them for 6 months or more before I sell them, though you did say somewhere else the tax people are cracking down on that?

Answer: There is no official minimum time that a taxpayer needs to be living in a property to make it qualify as their principal private residence (PPR). It is dependent on the 'quality of residence', i.e. the taxpayer needs to show that they moved in and resided with a 'degree of permanence, continuity or the expectation of continuity'.

Some tax advisers would advise six to twelve months of full occupation but other people would advise different amounts. See the Capital Gains Manual page CG64420 on the HM Revenue and Customs website:

http://www.hmrc.gov.uk/manuals/cgmanual/CG64420.htm

57.   Repairs to Commercial Property

Question: If a business rents a commercial property and has to replace part of the concrete floor in the warehouse to enable continued operations. Would this be an allowable expense?

Answer: If I understand you correctly, you are a tenant who runs a business from premises that you rent from a landlord, and you have to pay for the repair of the concrete floor. Your question is: is this payment an allowable business, revenue, expense that you can offset in full in the current year against your business profits? If you look on page PIM2020 on the   HMRC   Property   Income   Manual http://www.hmrc.gov.uk/manuals/pimmanual/PIM2020.htm you can see that a repair of a part of the structure of a property, when the replacement can be classified as 'like for like', i.e. without a significant upgrade or improvement to what was there originally, can be treated as a revenue, allowable business expense. This can be true even if the repairs are substantial.

58. NI Payments

Question: All of my income is from property letting and I submit a self-assessment return on the property section only to HMRC. I wondered what NI payments should be if any? I have always paid Class 2 only but it has been suggested that there may not be any liability.

Answer: Let me quote you from Tolleys: Property letting will rarely be regarded as self-employment for national insurance purposes, although if the extent of the landlord's involvement in managing the lettings and looking after the properties is substantial, it is possible that the activities will constitute a business, in which case Class 2 NI contributions will be payable. Class 4 contributions are only payable where income is taxed as trading income. Even though rents are now treated as being from a business in calculating property income, this is not the same as saying that a business actually exists, and it does not alter the national insurance position.

59. I Am Extending a Leasehold Flat Lease. Will There Be Anything Tax Deductible?

Question: Are all the costs and expenses associated with extending a lease on a leasehold flat tax deductible?

Answer: If you look on http://www.hmrc.gov.uk/manuals/pimmanual/PIM2025.htm you can see that the rent that a landlord has to pay to a superior landlord is an allowable expense. If you look on http://www.hmrc.gov.uk/manuals/pimmanual/PIM2205.htm you can see that a distinction is drawn between a lease of less than and more than 50 years. Although the context there is discussing the expense incurred by a landlord granting a lease to a tenant, I think that the distinction is still relevant to your scenario. If your lease that you are extending is for more than 50 years then I believe it is a capital expense and not allowable as a revenue expense against your rental income.

60. The Cost And Tax Implications of Separating Title Deeds

Question: My portfolio consists of 11 properties all under one Title Deed. I am now in a position where I need to separate some of these properties to have their own deeds. The business is a limited company. What are the costs and tax implications of separating these properties? Would it be of a benefit to have them under my own personal name, or to establish another Company?

Answer: It is beneficial ownership that counts for tax purposes, and pure legal ownership (as in the case of a bare trust) is not relevant. Therefore splitting the single title deed into separate ones, which is purely a legal ownership matter, and does not in any way affect the beneficial ownership, is not something that would trigger tax. However moving the properties out of the ownership of the company could trigger capital gains tax for the original company, and if you take the properties into your personal ownership, it could also trigger an income tax liability for you.

61. Would This Be Classed As An Equity Release Scheme?

Question: A relative aged 66 has no assets other than his house which is wholly owned and worth £150,000. I plan to gift him £500 per month. If he gifts me a share of the house, perhaps every 2 years, to compensate me in full - does this constitute an Equity Release Scheme which would impact his Pension Credit, etc.?

Answer: Any buyer and seller can claim that they are 'gifting' to each other, and that nothing commercial has taken place, but the reality is that a sale has happened.
It sounds to me that this is applicable to your scenario, and that there is either a sale here, or an Equity Release Scheme. Since calculation of Pension Credit takes into account the amount of capital the individual has over £10,000, it could impact on his entitlement to Pension Credit.

62. What Steps Can I Take With My Accountant And The Taxman?

Question: My wife and I jointly own a small number of buy-to-lets, and ten years ago my accountant completed a Form 17 declaration to HMRC to have the income allocated to my wife. Around six years ago, we bought three more buy-to-lets but did not complete further Form 17s although income continued to be allocated to my wife. The accountant mentioned this and I told him to advise me or just go and do it.

New senior management at the Accountants have advised me that I could be asked to pay tax at my higher tax rate. I am concerned that having employed a large accountancy firm and paid relatively high fees, I may now be expected to pay a large amount of back tax due to their errors. Is there any way forward on this?

Answer: In a case called Rowland v HMRC, the taxpayer claimed they relied on their accountant, who made a mistake. The taxpayer won and this was accepted as a 'reasonable excuse' (see HMRC Enquiry Manual: www.hmrc.gov.uk/manuals/emmanual/EM4110.htm. Page EM4110).

You can use this in your 'negotiations' with HMRC. I don't know all the details of your case but seems to me, from what you have written, you have a good argument to support your case.

63.   Will I Have to Pay Tax?

Question: I own a one bedroom property and intend to rent it out. There will be a difference between the mortgage payments on the property and the rent I am considering setting. Will I have to pay tax on this monetary difference? Also can I get an allowance from the taxman for any repairs I have to carry out?

Answer:

If the gross rent that you receive from your tenant, less the interest element of your mortgage payments, and less any allowable expenses that you incur, results in a positive figure, then this net figure is rental income which is taxable, and you will have to pay tax on it depending on the level of your other income in the tax year, and depending on your personal allowance.

From April 2017 there are going to be new rules for a residential property landlord claiming relief for interest paid to a lender.

64.   Claiming Mortgage Interest Relief On Buy-To-Let Property?

Question: During 2014 I took out £50,000 additional mortgage borrowing against my home residence and used this and savings to purchase a £81,000 buy-to-let property. I claimed tax relief on the £50,000 borrowing for my 2014-15 tax return, as the purpose was wholly and exclusively for business purposes. On 6th April 2015, I renewed my mortgage on my home residence (which included the £50,000) with a single fixed rate interest only mortgage of £135,000. I have no mortgage on my buy- to-let property which I own outright. Instead of £50,000 can I now claim mortgage interest tax relief for the full £81,000 purchase value of my buy-to-let property for my 2015-16 tax return?

Answer: If you look on http://www.hmrc.gov.uk/manuals/bimmanual/BIM45690.htm you can see that only the interest on the original amount that you actually borrowed to purchase the property (the £50,000) is allowable. The fact that you afterwards increased the mortgage on your home residence is not considered relevant to your property business, and the extra interest is therefore not allowable. So to make it clear, only 50/135 of your new interest cost is allowable.

65. Will We Be Subject To Income Tax?

Question: We are currently renting and wondered if we are able in some way of developing a property to then sell on for profit. During this time we will be living in both properties at the same time (paying council tax on both) as the 'project' is close to work.

Answer: When a person buys and develops a property in order to sell on at a profit then the profit is subject to income tax - it is deemed to be a trading venture. This applies even if the person lives in the property as their principal private residence at the same time. This can be seen on http://www.hmrc.gov.uk/manuals/cgmanual/CG65200.htm. Since it is a trade, Class 4 NI is also applicable.

66. As Joint Tenants Are We Forced To Split The Income 50%/50% for Tax Purposes?

Question: My wife and I own a property as Joint Tenants as opposed to Tenants in Common. Due to our respective incomes it would be more advantageous if we could apportion all of the income to my wife.

Answer: In order to achieve what you want, i.e. more of the rental income to be taxed in your wife's name, you need to do two things. Firstly you need to transfer a corresponding proportion of the property into your wife's name, either by formal conveyance, or by deed of trust to transfer beneficial ownership. Secondly within 60 days you need to complete a Form 17 (www.hmrc.gov.uk/forms/form17.pdf) and send it into HMRC together with proof of the transfer. The result of this will be your being taxed according to the actual proportion of the ownership, and not on a 50:50 basis.

67. What are the Tax Implications of Making Overpayments to My Mortgage?

Question: I would like to know what the tax implications are on making regular overpayments and/or 'lump sum' overpayments to pay off the capital on a 'buy to let' interest only mortgage.

Will I have to pay extra tax using this method if I were to use the 'excess monthly rent' as monthly overpayments once the monthly mortgage has been paid?

Answer: The answer to your question is very simple. Any interest payment you make to your mortgage lender is an allowable expense that can be offset against your gross rental income for calculating income tax.

Any capital repayment you make is not an allowable expense, and so cannot be offset against the gross rental income. Your mortgage lender should be able to tell you which payments you make are classified as interest payments and which are classified as capital repayments.

From April 2017 there are going to be new rules for a residential property landlord claiming relief for interest paid to a lender.

68. Is the Cost of Felling a Tree an Allowable Expense?

Question: Can you tell me whether the cost of felling a tree, that potential tenants (and certainly neighbours) were nervous of prior to tenanting taking place, be offset against rental income, as it was not just an improvement?

Answer: If the tree was posing a danger to the property then to pay for it to be felled would be an allowable expense.

69. Can Mortgage Interest Be Included On My Tax Return?

Question: My mortgage on the house I have been letting out is interest only. Can I put the full amount I pay each month in interest onto my tax return in the 'loan interest' section 24?

Answer: Yes, you can put the full amount you pay each month in interest (i.e. the annual amount) in the Property Income part of your tax return in the 'loan interest' section in box 24.

70. Tax On Rental Income

Question: Can I classify the total monthly mortgage repayment against total monthly rental, or only the interest element?

Answer: Only the interest element of the total monthly mortgage repayment can be treated as an allowable business expense to offset against your gross rental income. The remainder is a capital expense that reduces the original debt that you owe the lender, and is not relevant to your rental business.

From April 2017 there are going to be new rules for a residential property landlord claiming relief for interest paid to a lender.

71. Signing Over A Property To A Child

Question: What age does a child need to be for a parent to sign their property over them?

Answer: A child under the age of 18 cannot be a legal owner of property in this country. However they can have beneficial ownership, which is really what counts. So you can sign over beneficial ownership of a property to a child of any age, but if they are under 18, an adult will have to own it in trust for the child, the adult's name will have to be on the legal documents, and you will need a deed of trust to show the child's beneficial ownership.

72. What Is The Tax Position On Lender And Conveyancer Fees For Re-mortgages?

Question: I am remortgaging one of my buy-to-let properties, which incurs fees for the lender and the conveyancer. Are they in any way tax deductible?

Answer: You are remortgaging one of your buy to let properties, which incurs fees. I think you mean to say, this incurs fees for the borrower. If you look on page PIM2066 in the Property Income Manual on HMRC website (www.hmrc.gov.uk/manuals/pimmanual/PIM2066.htm) you can see that incidental costs incurred in obtaining loan finance, like arrangement fees, are allowable. So if the loan is allowable, which I presume it is, the fees incurred in setting up the loan are also allowable.

73. Can I Still Claim Tax Relief?

Question: I moved out of my residential property and took out an interest only buy to let mortgage and let out the property. After approximately 8 years I have moved back into the property (although I still have a second residence). Can I still claim the tax relief on the interest on the buy to let mortgage? Can I rent the property to myself to claim any tax relief?

Answer: Firstly, you cannot rent the property to yourself. Secondly, tax relief on the interest you pay your lender is only available to reduce your taxable rental income – if you have no rental income, it cannot be reduced. The interest you pay your lender cannot be offset against any other taxable income.

74. Do I Need to Inform HMRC About This Change?

Question: I have managed property for 15 years, mostly furnished but sometimes not and sometimes part. HMRC did not want me to keep changing from one to the other, so I maintained them all as furnished to get the 10% off rental income offset against tax. When does the property become unfurnished and require me to inform HMRC differently so that I do not get the 10% offset for all properties?

Answer: The 10% wear and tear allowance ceased 5 April 2016. However, it can be claimed before this date for fully furnished property.

75. How Do Capital Allowances Work for Small Commercial Property Investors?

Question: I purchased two freehold commercial properties for investment in 2011, one for approximately £130,000 and one for approximately £120,000. They are both occupied on commercial leases. They are both running as restaurants with flat above (one of which was sold on a long lease). Can I claim 25% of total purchase price of £250,000 which is £62,500 from HRMC and then another 25% later on for the period I hold these investments? Both are in my sole name. I am confused how capital allowances work for small time commercial property investors.

Answer: Capital allowances are available to the landlords of commercial property, but not on the whole property. They are only available on 'integral features' and certain special expenditure e.g. thermal insulation. Integral features include electrical (e.g. lighting) systems; cold water systems; space or water heating systems; powered systems of ventilation; air cooling or air purification (and any floor or ceiling comprised in such) systems; lifts, escalators and moving walkways; and external solar shading. From 2008-09 the rate of writing down allowance on these integral features of a building is the special rate of 10%, but from April 2012 it is 8%. This is calculated according to the reducing balance method – i.e. claim (e.g.) 10% the first year, then in the second year (e.g.) 8% of the 90% remaining from the first year, then in the third year 8% of the 82% remaining from the second year etc. I would advise you to get a valuation done – so that you know how much of the £250,000 you spent was attributable to the integral features, and how much was attributable to everything else. As regards the flats above – capital allowances are not available for dwelling houses; there are different rules that apply to them – e.g. the 10% wear and tear allowance.

76.   Is The Following Possible In Relation To Buy To Let?

Question: Before I set out on my whole buy to let venture are you able to confirm that the following is possible: a) I am able to raise through a loan the capital to purchase a buy to let from my residential property? b) I am able to claim tax relief on this load against my earnings on the rental property.

Answer: If you look on http://www.hmrc.gov.uk/manuals/bimmanual/BIM45685.htm you can see that as long as you use the borrowed money only for genuine business purposes, i.e. to buy the property to rent out, then all the interest you have to pay your lender is an allowable business expense that you can offset against your rental income for tax purposes. The fact that you borrow against your residential property doesn't matter - what is important is that you are using the funds for your business.

From April 2017 there are going to be new rules for a residential property landlord claiming relief for interest paid to a lender.

77.   What Is Our Tax Position?

I purchased a property jointly with my partner. We have equally funded the purchase. However, I borrowed £18,000 from my offset mortgage and we jointly have a £40,000 mortgage. My partner's daughter may occupy the property. Will there a tax liability? If so, what will be taken into account and how do I split this equally?

Answer: If you charge your partner's daughter a commercial rent, then the interest on the £18,000 and the £40,000 can be offset against the rental income. If you charge her less than a commercial rent, then there are special rules - see www.hmrc.gov.uk/manuals/pimmanual/PIM2220.htm   and www.hmrc.gov.uk/manuals/pimmanual/PIM4205.htm.

78.   Can I Offset Interest Payments?

Question: I own a flat which I let out to third party tenants. I took out a specific loan to purchase the flat which is completely separate from the loan I have on the property that I live in. Please can you confirm that the interest payments can be used in full to offset the rental income in my annual tax calculation?

Answer: The interest on the specific loan you to took out to purchase the flat which you let out is an allowable expense and the full amounts can be used to offset the rental income. See www.hmrc.gov.uk/manuals/pimmanual/PIM2105.htm.

From April 2017 there are going to be new rules for a residential property landlord claiming relief for interest paid to a lender.

79.   Is There A Tax Liability?

Question: I took a loan of my mortgage and invested the money elsewhere to get higher rate of interest. To explain with an example, I took withdrew £60,000 from my mortgage and put this money in a savings account which gives me 3% AER while my mortgage is 0.98%. Now I have to pay 0.98% on £60,000 to my bank. Do I pay tax on the difference? I.e. 3% less 0.98% or the entire 3% because I am paying interest (0.98%) on the loan anyway?

Answer: You are not a money lender running a money lending business, but an individual investor. Therefore you pay tax on the entire 3%, but the 0.98% is not an allowable expense to offset against the 3%.

80. Is This An Expense Or A Capital Charge?

Question: We have a property in the UK which is rented to students. Due to the nature of the type of tenant, the tenants tend to change each year. Is it right that the expense charged by our managing agents for drawing up this agreement cannot be charged as an expense, but rather as a capital charge? We have been renting out this property for 12 years on this basis so it's hardly a new enterprise.

Answer: If you look at http://www.hmrc.gov.uk/manuals/pimmanual/PIM2205.htm%20 you can see that if the let is for a year or less, then the legal expenses (such as the cost of drawing up a lease) and the agent's fees are not capital expenditure, and are therefore an allowable revenue expense.

81. Am I A Landlord Or Not?

Question: My wife and I jointly own my mother-in-law's flat which we inherited in 2005. In her will, the asset was to be shared also with my wife's brother and sister. By remortgaging (interest only) my present house I raised the funds to buy out the brother and sister. My wife and I now jointly own the flat with no mortgage and I have a mortgage on our home which is solely in my name. Since gaining ownership of the flat we have only ever let it, first to our son for several years and then to our daughter who is claiming housing benefit. We have never charged a commercial rent as the intention was to help them out. I have never declared this second property to HMRC. My mortgage comes to an end next year. What are my risks and liabilities and your advice for mitigating them please?

Answer: If you have received rental income from a property that you own, whether at a commercial rate or below it, then you are obligated to inform HMRC. The exception to this rule is in a situation when both of the following conditions apply: a) You are not liable to tax on the rental income, either because the amount is covered by your income tax personal allowance (you don't have other income using up your personal allowance); or because your allowable expenses on the property equal or exceed the rent. b) Your gross rental income (before deducting allowable expenses) is less than £10,000 per annum, and your net rental income is less than £2,500 per annum. See:

www.hmrc.gov.uk/sa/introduction.htm#1. If you look back over your records from the past years and you find that you owe tax to HMRC, then the best thing is for you to approach them first, before they approach you.

82.   Can I Claim Outgoings Against Rental Income?

Question: I had a lifetime mortgage of £70,000 on my private residence and in January 2012 I borrowed a further £50,000 to pay off a buy to let mortgage on my flat. Can I now claim my whole monthly mortgage outgoings against rental income?

Answer: Look at www.hmrc.gov.uk/manuals/bimmanual/BIM45685.htm where you can see that if the purpose of the loan is to fund the business (in this case - the rental property) it doesn't matter that the security for the loan is the taxpayer's private residence. Here the new £50,000 loan is just replacing and standing in the shoes of the original buy to let mortgage, the interest on which was allowable. But you cannot claim the whole monthly mortgage outgoings - the interest on the old £70,000 loan is not allowable.

83.   Is This A Tax Deductible Expense?

Question: I have a really old bathroom in my let property, over 15 years old. I want to take it out and install a new bathroom for the new tenants, totally decorate and upgrade. Is this tax deductible?

Answer: Here is a quote from HMRC's property income manual (www.hmrc.gov.uk/manuals/pimmanual/PIM2020.htm): "Even if the repairs are substantial, that does not of itself make them capital for tax purposes, provided the character of the asset remains unchanged. For example, if a fitted kitchen is refurbished the type of work carried out might include the stripping out and replacement of base units, wall units, sink etc., re-tiling, work top replacement, repairs to floor coverings and associated re-plastering and re-wiring. Provided the kitchen is replaced with a similar standard kitchen then this is a repair and the expenditure is allowable. If at the same time additional cabinets are fitted, increasing the storage space, or extra equipment is installed, then this element is a capital addition and not allowable (applying whatever apportionment basis is reasonable on the facts). But if the whole kitchen is substantially upgraded, for example if standard units are replaced by expensive customised items using high quality materials, the whole expenditure will be capital. There is no longer any relief for 'notional repairs', which is the notional cost of the repairs that would otherwise have had to be carried out."

84.   What's The Tax Position On Rental Income Received By Joint Owners?

Question: We are 3 brothers who own a house which is rented out. Does the rent received have to be divided between us for tax reasons or is it possible for one or two of us to have it only on our books?

Answer: You are allowed to come to an agreement, preferably written and before the start of the tax year that the rental income will be received in a different proportion to the ownership of the property. Make sure that the rental income is only received in the right bank accounts according to the rental agreement. See hmrc.gov.uk/manuals/pimmanual/PIM1030.htm.

85.   How Far Back Will HMRC Go To Assess My Income Tax Liability?

Question: I have been renting out a property for about 8 years through a letting agency. I assumed that the letting agency was dealing with the tax aspects and so never sent in an income tax return. I recently became aware that I should send in a tax return and would like to know how far back the HMRC will want to assess my income.

Answer: The first thing is to make a calculation for each of the last 8 tax years separately to see whether a) you have actually made a net profit from your rental business (i.e. that your rental income is more than your allowable expenses), and b) that those profits are subject to tax (e.g. they are not covered by personal allowances or brought forward rental losses). If after these calculations you find that you owe tax to HMRC then your best option is to contact HMRC (before they contact you!) on the voluntary disclosure helpline on 0845 601 5041.

86.   What Do I Have To Do To Qualify?

Question: I have my own company that trades in a non-property area, and also have a series of buy to let properties that are owned in my own name. I have read on HMRC's website of 'entrepreneurs' relief' at 10% and I am interested in understanding how I can qualify for this rate and what do I have to do to qualify.

Answer: See www.hmrc.gov.uk/manuals/cgmanual/CG63980.htm that a buy to let property business does not qualify for entrepreneurs' relief (ER). But assuming the other conditions are complied with, the shares in your non property trading company should be eligible for ER.

87.   When Is The Tax Due?

Question: I bought a property in December 2011 and rented my previous house. The buy to let mortgage was taken out on my previous house from December 2011. My previous house was rented from May 2012 to date. How will the tax be worked out? Will it be from the date that I rented the property or from the date the mortgage was taken out? Also I have a repayment buy to let mortgage, is this a good idea or shall I change it to interest only? I also did a driveway so that the tenants can park the car, is this an allowable expense?

Answer: See HMRC's guidance (www.hmrc.gov.uk/manuals/pimmanual/PIM2505.htm) that a property business begins when it first receives income, which would be May 2012 in your case. You were paying interest from December 2011, which could be argued to be a pre trading expense. However I think it is more likely to be classified as 'Interest payable on property only partly used for rental business', about which you should read www.hmrc.gov.uk/manuals/pimmanual/PIM2105.htm. With regard to the mortgage, whichever kind you have, it is only the interest element that is allowable for tax, and not the capital repayment element. About the driveway, if there was a driveway there before, and you just repaired it, then that would be an allowable expense, but if there was no driveway before and you put one in, then that is called an improvement, and classified as a capital expense, which can only be offset against the capital gain when you sell the property. See www.hmrc.gov.uk/manuals/pimmanual/PIM2020.htm.

88.   What Is My Tax Position And Should I Form A Company?

Question: I have two properties that I let out. Should I just add the rental income to my full time salary of around £42,000 (+ 18,000 (rental income) = £60,000) on the self-assessment form? Therefore approximately £15,000 will be taxable and charged at 40% = £6,000 tax leaving me £9,000; and will I have to pay National Insurance contributions (NICs) on the rental income as I put it through self-assessment? Would it be better to set up a partnership or company? Both properties are held in unequal shares (tenants in common) with my partner.

Answer: You should put the £18,000 on the UK Property supplementary pages of the self-assessment return, and not just add it to your salary income. There is no NICs on this property income. If your partner is not a higher rate taxpayer there is something simple and legitimate that you can do to push more property income into the hands of your partner and overall pay less income tax. And if that idea is not suitable there is something else that you can do, again simple and legitimate, to push property income into the hands of a limited company, and consequently pay less tax overall. Speak to a tax adviser.

89.   Is This A 'Wasting Asset'?

Question: I recently purchased a leasehold property and the original lease was 99 years of which 10 years are left. I paid £100,000 to the existing leaseholder for the assignment of lease in my favour for right to use property for the next 10 years. Would this be classed as a wasting asset and if yes what is the correct tax treatment please?

Answer: Of the £100,000 received by the existing lease holder, (10 - 1) = 9 years at 2% = 18% is treated as a part disposal for capital gains purposes. The remaining £82,000 is treated as rental income in his hands. You can claim this £82,000 as a deduction in calculating your taxable profits, but spread over 10 years, i.e. £8,200 per year.

90.   When Can I Claim For These Required Repairs?

Question: I purchased a grade 2 listed cottage and have been given a schedule of items by the local council, listing the required repairs, but they must be in the old type of materials for roof, windows, etc. so there is no 'enhancement'. Some textbooks state that one is allowed to claim some repairs costs before starting to receive rental income, as long as they are just repairs and not enhancements, whereas other text books state that no expenditure prior to rental is allowed against rental income, only against future capital gains. In your opinion would any of these required repairs be allowable against future rental income?

Answer: If you look on www.hmrc.gov.uk/manuals/pimmanual/PIM2505.htm you can see that an expense incurred before starting to rent out can be allowable. Also if you look at www.hmrc.gov.uk/manuals/pimmanual/PIM2020.htm you can see that a distinction is made when doing repairs to a newly bought property before starting to rent it out, between whether the property was fit to be rented out when bought, or whether it wasn't. If not fit, then the repairs are classified as capital expenses, and can only be claimed against future capital gains when the property is sold.

91.   How Does A Deed Of Trust Work?

Question: I understand it is possible to get a buy to let mortgage in my own name (to benefit from the better mortgage deals available to individuals) but then transfer the 'beneficial' ownership of the property to a limited property company owned by myself, by means of a deed of trust? Can you explain how a deed of trust works in this instance and how to set one up? I'm assuming the property will stay in my name at the land registry. Also, I don't think I have to inform my mortgage lender about this (is this correct?). For accounting purposes, I assume that all the rent and expenses, etc. will just show through the company's accounts as though the company were the legal owner of the asset.

Answer: You can obtain from a solicitor or someone else a pro forma deed of trust that says 'that until now A was the legal and beneficial owner of the asset, but now he is transferring the beneficial ownership (or a percentage of it) to B'. Re your mortgage lender: this is not a tax question and you really need to speak to someone with legal knowledge, but it seems to me that if you don't first inform your mortgage lender about the transfer of the beneficial ownership then it could be considered to be mortgage fraud. On the assumption that you do successfully transfer the beneficial ownership to the company and you remain purely as a bare trustee, then you are correct - all the rent and expenses will show through the company's accounts.

92.   Can I Utilise Loss Relief?

Question: My wife and I own 100% of four UK properties (2 each) and my properties are making losses whilst my wife's are okay. We want to utilise rental losses in a tax efficient way and not have to worry about capital gains tax, etc. Would my wife be able to transfer 100% of her property to me so that I can utilise my prior and present losses? Would the outcome be the same if my wife transferred 50% instead of 100%?

Answer: If you look at www.hmrc.gov.uk/manuals/pimmanual/PIM4205.htm and www.hmrc.gov.uk/manuals/pimmanual/PIM4210.htm you can see that rental business losses can be offset against profits from the same rental business, either in the same year or carried forward to a future year. If you expand your rental business by obtaining new (profit making) properties while at the same time continuing your present rental business, then that is considered to be the same rental business, and the old brought forward losses can be set off against the new profits, for tax purposes.

But your wife would need to make a proper, bona fide transfer to you of the properties (or at least the beneficial ownership of the properties) for this to work.

The same would apply if she only transferred 50% of her properties to you, but then of course only 50% of the profits would be available to you for offset. If it is acceptable to you to receive only 50% of the profits, then an alternative is for her to transfer even a minimal amount of the properties to you, e.g. 5%. If you **DO NOT** send in a Form 17, since you and your wife together own the properties, then due to the 50:50 rule half the property income will be deemed to be yours for tax purposes, and consequently available to you for offset. See www.hmrc.gov.uk/manuals/tsemmanual/TSEM9800.htm.

93.   Tax Relief On Mortgage Payments - How Far Back Can I Go?

Question: How many years can I go back to claim back the tax relief on the interest I have paid on mortgage payments for my buy-to-let properties? I am a 40% taxpayer.

Answer: If income tax, corporation tax or capital gains tax has been paid and the taxpayer believes that the payment was excessive it is possible to make a claim for overpayment relief if no other statutory steps are available and the taxpayer has used any available rights of appeal. This claim must be made within four years after the end of the relevant tax year or accounting period.

94.   Property Held On Trust For A Company?

Question: I have a limited company. I purchased a buy-to-let flat and it is registered at the Land Registry in my personal name. The purchase price was £150,000 and I financed this with a £70,000 mortgage in my personal name. I paid cash for the difference (£80,000). My intention is to have long-term rental income for my pension. I signed a Trust Deed with the solicitors at the time of purchase of the flat and I am the trustee. The trust deed records that I (as trustee) acknowledge that I hold the property on trust for the grantee (the company) and that all income from the property shall belong to the grantee. Should the flat be reflected as a fixed asset in the financial statements of the company? Should the £70,000 mortgage be reflected as a long term liability in the financial statements of the company? Should the £80,000 cash deposit be reflected as a shareholder loan in the financial statements of the company? Can I claim the interest on the mortgage as an expense in the company?

Answer: From what you have described it seems to me that the property should be reflected as a fixed asset in the financial statements of the company, since your trust deed clearly indicates so. I suggest that the company should show that it owes you £150,000. However, the mortgage is in your own name. The interest you pay your lender therefore cannot be a company expense. I suggest that you draw up a loan agreement and charge your company interest equivalent to the interest you have to pay to your lender. That interest will be allowable for the company. The interest you pay should also be able to be classified as 'allowable interest' - see Box 5 on page 2 of the SA101 self-assessment return form.

95. Can I Offset The Interest On The Loan Against The Rental Property?

Question I raised a loan by remortgaging the jointly owned family home and buying a student rental property outright. The mortgage is interest only and in joint names of my husband and me. The purchased rental property is in my sole name and I manage that property. I understood from a local accountant that I can offset the interest on the loan against the rental property as it was a loan raised to purchase that property, is this correct? Also, the rent is at the moment paid into a joint bank account, but the profit, after all the mortgage is paid and any allowable expenses etc., are paid out, is transferred into an account in my sole name. Would it be better if the rent was paid directly into an account in my sole name initially? My husband is a higher rate earner and the rental property was to help provide me with some sort of pension in the future, as at the moment I only have the state pension to look forward to!

Answer: What your accountant told you is correct, since the loan was raised to purchase the rental property, interest on the remortgage can be offset against the rental income. However, since it is a joint mortgage, only half the interest is your responsibility, and therefore only your half of the interest can be offset against the rental income. This may cause you a problem. Perhaps you can attempt to renegotiate the mortgage in some way (e.g. make it totally in your name, with your husband acting as a guarantor). Alternatively, make your husband a partial owner of the property. Fix his percentage ownership of the property at a level where the amount of rental income he receives exactly equals the amount of interest he pays. This way, his net rental income is nil, and he pays no tax. You will need a Form 17 for this. If you decide to retain 100% of the ownership, it doesn't matter if the rental income goes into a joint account; since your husband has no ownership in the property, HMRC can have nothing to say.

96.   Can We Split The Rental Profit This Way?

Question: My wife, son and I have just purchased a property in Scotland in our joint names - one-third each. My wife and I only wish to cover our interest on the loan that we have taken out to purchase the property, with our son receiving the balance of the rental profit. Is it possible to do this?

Answer: Assuming your son is over 18, yes it is possible to do so. Draw up a written income agreement saying that even though the ownership of the property is one third each, nevertheless the income is entitled to be received in a different proportion. Then make sure that the right amount of income actually goes to a single name bank account for that individual. The taxation will follow the entitlement to the rental income, as per the agreement.

97.   Are These Modernisations Capital Or Revenue Costs?

Question: I have recently bought a property that has needed full modernisation –double-glazed windows, carpets, bathroom, kitchen, painting, boiler replacement, etc. Is this all treated as a capital cost as it is pre-tenancy or can it be treated as a revenue expense? Tenants will move in the day after the work is completed.

Answer: Look at www.hmrc.gov.uk/manuals/pimmanual/PIM2020.htm where you can see that the crucial questions to ask are: a) was the property not in a fit state for rental use before the refurbishment was carried out? or b) was the price paid for the property substantially reduced because of its dilapidated state? If yes, then the refurbishment costs are capital expenditure.

98.   Do You Have To Split Income According To Ownership?

Question: One son is a student who owns 50% of the house he was living in with three tenants. My husband and I own 25% each. We were told by accountants and then by an HMRC adviser at a Landlord Expo that we had to split income according to ownership. I now read in 'How to Avoid Landlord Taxes' that this can be changed. Is it too late to change for previous tax year (2012/13) and how would we do that? Do utility bills and other expenses (advertising for tenants comes to mind) have to be split the same way? Is it possible to allocate the wear and tear allowance in a different way from the income, i.e. not to offset it against our son's income?

Answer: It is too late to change things for the tax year 2012/13. When a property is owned in partnership, the normal method of computation of taxable income and allowable tax deductions (e.g. utility bills, advertising and the wear and tear allowance) is to make a calculation for the property as a whole, until you get down to the net profit figure for the whole property. This net figure is then split according to the partner profit sharing agreement. In the absence of an explicit profit sharing agreement, the net profit is split according to the underlying ownership of the property. However, obviously if one of the partners suffered an expense that the others did not (e.g. he had to borrow money and therefore pay interest in order to fund his investment, and the other partners did not need to), then only he would claim this expense.

99.   Can My Daughter Be On The Deeds Even Though She's Not Paid A Penny?

Question: My girlfriend (partner) and I have re-mortgaged and using savings are going through the process of buying a house with a view to letting it. Would it be possible to purchase the house in my partner's and daughter's name only, as I wish her to own at least part of the house for her future and in the meantime my partner to receive the rent as she is a non-taxpayer? What concerns me is if I put my daughter's name on the deeds for the house to let will it be queried that she has not contributed any of the payment towards the purchase? I am a higher rate taxpayer so would not want to be on the deeds.

Answer: Firstly, if you look at www.hmrc.gov.uk/manuals/cgmanual/CG34400.htm you can see that if someone buys an asset in the name of their child, HMRC accept that the asset is beneficially owned by the child, even though the parent paid for it. However, for income tax purposes, since you paid for the house, then under the 'settlement' rules, if the income from the property is more than £100 per year the income will be deemed to be yours and not that of your child, and you will be taxed accordingly. From what I understand, you and your partner are not married. So if you and your partner owned the property (and not your child and your partner) then you could overcome the income tax problem by making a written partnership agreement with your partner that all the property rental income should go to her. Then make sure it is actually paid into an account in her individual name (see www.hmrc.gov.uk/manuals/pimmanual/PIM1030.htm). This would ensure that your partner is taxed on all the rental income. However, in your situation, even though you, as a parent, are taxed on your child's income, I am unsure whether, from a legal perspective, you are allowed to 'give away' the child's rental income to your partner. If you can clarify the legal situation, then the tax treatment should follow.

100. Can I Revalue To Save Tax?

Question: I have a rental property that is now worth less than I paid for it. Can I 'revalue it' without selling it, and can I offset this loss against other income to save tax?

Answer: A revaluation is not an expense that is allowable for tax purposes. Firstly, no actual transaction has occurred, it is just a book entry. Secondly, it is a capital matter, which cannot be classified as a revenue expense.

101. Would Our Tax Liability Be Affected?

Question: We will soon be renting out our residential property due to moving overseas for work. I know that the interest only part of our mortgage payment attracts tax relief, but if we put some or all of the remaining rental income into an offset or overpayment account with our mortgage provider, would that affect our tax liability?

Answer: This is a quote from a lending bank: 'An offset mortgage links your current and savings account balances to your mortgage in order to reduce the mortgage balance you're charged interest on. So, if your mortgage balance is £125,000 and you have £25,000 in your linked current and savings accounts, we'd calculate your monthly mortgage interest on £100,000 instead of the full mortgage balance of £125,000. You can use the offset savings in one of two ways: (1) Reduce your mortgage payments. The interest you save in one month by offsetting could reduce your mortgage payment the following month. (2) Reduce your mortgage term. Keep your monthly mortgage payments the same and pay off your mortgage sooner.' If you choose the first option, and consequently make smaller monthly interest payments, your net taxable profit will consequently be larger, so your tax bill should be higher. But there are other factors to take into account, eg. whether you are eligible for a UK income tax personal allowance, and how much is your total UK income.

102.   Is This Replacement An Allowable Expense?

Question: I have been letting my property for eight years and would like to replace my wooden double glazed windows for uPVC double glazed windows as the wooden ones are in a poor state and two of them cannot be opened. Is this an allowable expense or not?

Answer: Please look in www.hmrc.gov.uk/manuals/pimmanual/PIM2020.htm, especially at the end of the page, and you can understand that this can be called a replacement of 'like for like', and allowable as a revenue expense to offset against your rental income.

103.   Do I Have To Pay Tax On The Money I Receive After A Property Buy-Out?

Question: My partner has an agreement from our building society to re-mortgage our currently jointly owned home, in effect buying me out. I will transfer ownership to him and take a sum of money from the re-mortgage. The amount I receive will be about £45,000 and I wondered will I have to pay any tax on this?

Answer: From what I understand you are not married. If so, your sale of your half of the house to your partner will be subject to capital gains tax, if the amount you sell to your partner for is more than the original price paid for your half. However since you live in the property (you mentioned it is your home) most probably you have principal private residence relief available to you, so that you don't pay any tax.

104.   Who Takes The Cost Of The Mortgage And Other Costs?

Question: My husband and I are the legal owners of a buy-to-let property. We want to give each of our two children a 20% share in the beneficial ownership whilst leaving the mortgage in our joint names as neither child is yet earning, though both are over 18. Would the children as beneficial owners need each to set 20% of the mortgage/other cost against their income or do we take all the cost because the loan is in our joint names and we are legal owners?

Answer: Since the mortgage is in your names and not those of your children, only you can set the mortgage interest against your rental income. As for other costs, such as insurance and repairs, it depends who decides to pay for them - it would seem that you have more flexibility in these matters than the mortgage interest.

105.   How Should We Split The Ownership?

Question: My partner and I are purchasing a property together. I am in full-time employment, he is re-training and has just gone self-employed and is currently not utilising his single person's tax allowance. However, I am paying the 25% deposit. How should we divide the ownership of the property to maximise any tax relief?

Answer: From the wording of your question "My partner and I" I get the impression that you are not married. If so, you can divide up the actual ownership of the property in whichever proportion you want, and then make a written agreement between you (preferably before you start renting out the property) that the rental income will be received in a different proportion - one that utilises your partners' personal allowance and the basic rate band of both of you in the most efficient way. Then make sure that the rental income actually goes to your individual bank accounts according to the pre-agreed amounts.

106.   Are HMRC Correct?

Question: I was instructed by Nottingham City council as part of the House in Multiple Occupation (HMO) licensing scheme to fit 'Grade A' fire alarm and emergency lighting systems in my properties. HMRC are now saying that they are not allowable as a taxable deduction - are they correct?

Answer: In my opinion perhaps they mistakenly construed this expenditure as capital expenditure. But actually it is revenue expenditure. It is not exactly the same, but similar to that which can be seen on www.hmrc.gov.uk/manuals/bimmanual/BIM47310.htm that an alarm system and floodlighting are qualifying assets, and this is not affected by the fact that the assets may become fixed to land.

107.   Can We Claim Tax Relief On The Interest?

Question: I currently own a house worth about £300,000 with an outstanding mortgage of about £50,000 which is solely in my name. I am thinking of remortgaging, for about

£160,000, to buy a second property to rent out. I will be taking out the new mortgage jointly (between myself and my wife) to offset tax between the two of us, I am a higher rate taxpayer and she has no current income. My current mortgage company have no issue in lending us the money for this purpose. But my question is with it being a mortgage on our current residence and not on the buy-to-let, or a buy-to-let mortgage, can we still claim the tax relief on the interest?

Answer: If you look at HMRC's Property Income manual (at www.hmrc.gov.uk/manuals/bimmanual/BIM45685.htm), you can see that since the loan is taken out for the purpose of your property business, the interest incurred is an allowable expense and it doesn't matter that the security for the loan is your own personal home.

108. What Constitutes Repairs To The Property Or An Improvement?

Question: I have a receipt from a tradesman who did some work for me in my rented out property. The receipt says "remove and dispose of existing bathroom. Replace bathroom with shower and small bathroom fittings." There was a bath originally and the room itself a bit dated. The bath has been replaced with a shower and made more presentable to help with re-letting the property.

Answer: If you look at HMRC's Property Income manual (at www.hmrc.gov.uk/manuals/pimmanual/PIM2020.htm), you can see how HMRC distinguishes between an improvement and a replacement of 'like for like'. From what you have described it would seem that your case is similar to the replacement of an old kitchen by an equivalent kitchen, detailed at the end of that page, and therefore is a revenue expense, allowable against rental income.

109. What Costs Are Allowable?

Question: Please can you explain what costs can be offset against income at the initial purchase stage of a property? Costs such as mortgage product fees, broker and valuation fees etc., plus solicitors costs can be substantial. I understand that all re-mortgage costs can be offset; however, is it the same at start-up for new purchase costs?

Answer: If you look at HMRC's Property Income manual (at www.hmrc.gov.uk/manuals/pimmanual/PIM2205.htm), you can see that costs relating to the purchase of a property are capital expenses and cannot be offset against rental income. However if you look at www.hmrc.gov.uk/manuals/pimmanual/PIM2066.htm, you can see that the costs involved in setting up a mortgage are allowable against rental income, in the same way as interest on the mortgage.

110. Can You Advise Me On What I Should Do For The Best?

Question: I found an article on your website (www.taxinsider.co.uk/876-How to Pay off Your Main Residence Mortgage And Claim Tax Relief.html) and I have a few issues: (1) I called the tax office in 2003 about this and they said I could not claim interest for a second property to fund the capital value of my first property. I have phoned since and they said I could not claim, then when I mentioned the rule they said I needed to write in. (2) I understand that I can request a copy of all correspondence/details of conversations held on HMRC's file, since I have nothing. What do you suggest? At the moment I have not paid any taxes, as there are tax losses, so there is no tax to be refunded, only unclaimed interest tax relief to increase my losses carried forward. What should I do: (a) add prior years' unclaimed tax on my next tax return and leave a note; (b) write to HMRC for a copy of conversations held with them to confirm their incorrect answer to me (our last conversation we had was that they continue to deny I can claim this interest); or (c) calculate the interest relief and ask for guidance to add to next year's return or amend current year return?

Answer: If you borrow money in order to fund the purchase of a rental property, then the interest is always allowable, even if the security on the loan is your main residence - see www.hmrc.gov.uk/manuals/bimmanual/BIM45685.htm. If you have made losses you must register them with HMRC. Write to HMRC, either separately, or through a note on your tax return, in order to register your brought forward rental losses.

111. Do I Need To Pay Tax Twice?

Question: How should I best deal with income from property in the United States, which has paid property tax in the US but was earned by a UK national resident in the UK? I assume that it should be declared to HMRC but the US tax paid is deducted from the income tax due. What are the best ways to minimize the overall tax burden?

Answer: You have to declare the US rental income on the SA106 (Foreign) supplementary pages of the self-assessment return www.hmrc.gov.uk/forms/sa106.pdf. You should claim foreign tax credit relief in the section dealing with property income - see HMRC Helpsheet 263, so that you do not pay tax twice.

112. Can I Claim The Repairs On My Tax Return?

Question: I have a rental property and had a major flood in it last year, resulting in the cancellation of lots of bookings. I paid out about £20,000 for repairs to the property. However, I did not claim on my insurance. I am trying to claim for all the repairs on my tax return by stating that it was simply replacing what was originally there. Is this the correct procedure?

Answer: It is the correct procedure. As long as you are only restoring the property to its original position, and not making improvements, this is an allowable expense. See www.hmrc.gov.uk/manuals/pimmanual/PIM2020.htm and www.hmrc.gov.uk/briefs/income-tax/brief0513.htm.

113. Joint Ownership Or Gifting Properties - What Is The Best Option?

Question: My wife (lower rate taxpayer) and I (higher rate taxpayer) are looking at buying a few more buy-to-let properties. Our eldest daughter is 18; the other two are under 18. Is it beneficial for these new properties to be in my wife, eldest daughter and my name? Would this split the profits three ways? What about the other two children - should we do anything now or wait until they become 18?

Answer: It is a good idea to make all five family members own a share of the property now. However, any income attributable to those under 18 will be taxed on the parents. Between the three children over 18, you could draw up a written income agreement giving more income to your daughter (i.e. a bigger percentage share of the income than her share of ownership of the property). This will enable the rental income to be taxed at lower rates (presumably she has little other income) and will also perhaps help to support her at this stage of her life (e.g. through university).

114. Can I Claim Interest Relief On These Borrowings?

Question: I have purchased several buy-to-let properties using my own home as security. Some of the buy-to-let properties are registered and income declared in my own name, and others I have put into a limited company. Am I entitled to claim interest relief on my borrowings?

Answer: Yes you are.

See www.hmrc.gov.uk/manuals/pimmanual/PIM2105.htm that states interest is an allowable expense. And note (see www.hmrc.gov.uk/manuals/bimmanual/BIM45685.htm) that this applies also when you use your own home as security. However, you must make sure that the loans for the properties owned by the company are company loans, and not personal loans, because if they are personal loans the interest is not allowable. There is a way round this problem, but perhaps you would need to speak to a tax adviser about 'qualifying loan interest' - see www.hmrc.gov.uk/worksheets/sa101-notes.pdf%20at%20page%20AiN20.

From April 2017 there are going to be new rules for a residential property landlord claiming relief for interest paid to a lender.

115.   Should We Move The Property Into A Company?

Question: My wife and I own a commercial property, currently rented out, but the tenants have a right to buy. If we sell there will be a capital gain of around £100,000. Could we move the property into a company in exchange for shares to hold over the capital gains until the shares are sold?

Answer: There is no holdover relief for an investment property unless it is a qualifying furnished holiday let, or it is disposed of under a compulsory purchase order. If someone is incorporating a trading business, and the property from which the business traded was going into the company, then holdover of the capital gain on the property in exchange for shares could apply.

116.   Property Owned By A Minor - Can This Be Done?

Question: I co-own a business. We recently transferred the business from an LLP to a company. I have a director's account in my company, but once that is exhausted I'll be a higher rate taxpayer again. We are accumulating capital in the business (about £300,000 last time I looked). We have bought all the kit we need for the business and cleared all loans. I now want to start investing in property to rent out, and to hold for years while the value climbs (as it seems to be starting to again). My business partner and I might do this as a company project, but for the time being his personal circumstances mean he doesn't want to complicate his 'share' of the business with property. I could take out £120,000 to buy a property for rental and I've seen one that would be ideal. My son is 14 and in private education and I have the following questions: (1) Can I buy this property in his name (my wife and I as legal owners, son as beneficial owner)? (2) Can rental revenue then be paid into an account in his name to minimise the tax burden? (3) Can that account then be used to pay his school fees?

Answer: You can certainly buy the property with you and your wife the legal owners and your son as the beneficial owner. However, due to the 'settlements' anti-avoidance legislation, annual income from any asset owned by an unmarried minor bought by the parents' capital is taxed, for income tax purposes, on the parents, if the annual income is more than £100 per parent per tax year. But maybe it is still worth it for you because when he becomes 18 this rule won't apply any more.

117.   Can I Gift My Half Share?

Question: I own a half share in a property which I don't live in. I have my own property in another part of the country. Can I gift my half share without financial implications? For example, can I gift it to a charity? I would like to 'get rid' of my half share for various family reasons, so just need to know how I can do this without financial implications.

Answer: If you gift your half share in the property, for capital gains tax purposes you are deemed to have disposed of it at its present market value, even though when you gift you receive no money. www.hmrc.gov.uk/manuals/cgmanual/CG14530.htm. Therefore if it is worth more now than its value when you acquired it, you have made a capital gain. However when you gift to a charity, it is deemed to be 'no gain no loss' i.e. you are deemed not to have made any capital gain. www.hmrc.gov.uk/manuals/cgmanual/CG66621.htm.

118.   How Can We Reduce The Amount Of Tax We Pay Back?

Question: My sister and I jointly own an ex-council property that was left to us by my father when he passed away in 2000. Since then, we have renovated it and have from time to time rented it out. At the moment I am living there during the week, as it is local to where I work. We have been thinking about selling it for some time, but the capital gains tax we would have to pay has put us off. In 2000 it was roughly valued at £100,000 (per the inheritance form). We would like to cash in whilst the market in London is buoyant. It is now valued at around £390,000-450,000. How can we reduce the amount of tax we pay? Are there ways round this? How do we stand legally, etc.?

Answer: I have no answer for your sister, but for you it would be beneficial to elect to make the house your principal private residence (PPR), even if only for a short time. See www.hmrc.gov.uk/manuals/cgmanual/CG64510.htm. This will enable you to claim a) PPR relief for the period of actual occupation and also the last 18 months of ownership (for a sale after 5 April 2014) (if the two periods don't overlap), and also b) the letting exemption to reduce the gain attributable to the period when the house was let out. This will reduce the capital gain on your half of the house.

119. Do I Need To Include This In My Self-Assessment Form?

Question: If one owns a property jointly and it is not being let at present, but is occupied by a family member who pays the outgoings, does one still have to inform the tax office on one's return? And can one of the joint owners be elected as the owner responsible for declaring income when it is let in the future?

Answer: If in a tax year you do not receive any rental income you do not need to inform HM Revenue & Customs on a tax return. If joint owners receive rental income from a property (e.g. four people receive a quarter each), then each one is responsible for declaring his quarter on his own tax return - one of the joint owners cannot be made responsible to declare on behalf of all of them.

120. Are There Any Tax Implications We Need To Be Aware Of?

Question: A friend has offered me the chance to purchase a house which is on sale for £200,000 and is the same price as it was bought at 8 years ago. The market value is £350,000-£385,000. My question is two-fold – is it okay for my friend to sell it at less than the market value; and what are the tax implications for each of us, if any? My friend has another home which is his principal place of residence.

Answer: See www.hmrc.gov.uk/manuals/cgmanual/CG14530.htm, where it is explained that if: "The transaction is otherwise than by way of a bargain at arm's length" then HMRC have the right to substitute market value for the consideration i.e. what is agreed between the seller and buyer and actually paid. Since the consideration here of £200,000 is so much less than the market value, you stand a serious risk of HMRC claiming that this is not just a 'bad sale' by the seller, but that the property was sold cheaply because the buyer and seller are friends etc., and consequently for capital gains tax purposes they will use the market value of £350,000-£385,000. The result will be that the seller must pay capital gains tax on £350,000-£385,000 less the purchase price of £200,000. But the buyer will be able to use the market value figure of £350,000-£385,000 as his acquisition base cost in any future capital gains tax computation when he sells on the property in the future.

121. What Are Our Tax Positions?

Question: My husband and I are soon to buy another buy-to-let flat in London (we are currently not resident in UK, and won't be for another 5-10 years. We are able to claim personal allowance, given our UK nationality). We are considering buying the flat in our names plus those of our two young children (each with a 25% share) using 'joint tenants' ownership. My husband and I would advise HMRC that we are to receive rental income 50:50 between us (so no rent to our children, given they wouldn't enjoy personal allowance on any income from us). So there is no short-term income tax benefit. However, at time of sale I assume we could all share the capital gain at 25% each, thus hopefully reducing overall tax rate on total gain. Do you agree in principle? Are there any other points we should consider here?

Answer: See www.hmrc.gov.uk/manuals/tsemmanual/TSEM4300.htm where you can see, as apparently you wrote, that when the parent supplies the capital, then the income produced is deemed, for income tax purposes, to be that of the parent. However this does not apply for capital gains. So even though you supplied the capital, when the property is eventually sold the sale proceeds will be attributed 25% to each member of the family, and your children will get their capital gains annual exemption, as can be seen at www.hmrc.gov.uk/manuals/cgmanual/CG18010.htm (re the annual exemption).

122. Tenants-In-Common And Property - What Will Be The Tax Position?

Question: My husband and I held our house as tenants-in-common. He died in 1988 and left his share to our daughter. I now wish to sell the house and move nearer to my daughter; she lives 100 miles away. Will she have to pay any tax on the sale?

Answer: Yes, she will have to pay capital gains tax on her half of the house, based on the difference between the value in 1988 when she inherited from her father, and today's sale proceeds. I am making an assumption that she never lived in the house as her principal private residence, because if she did at one time, then that changes the picture considerably.

123. Rental Income Losses – Can I Offset?

Question: I realise that such losses can normally only be offset against profits on rented property. However, what is the position if I sell the property I rent out, but there are remaining losses which I therefore cannot offset in the future? Can I then offset these against my income, which is all from pensions or do I simply have to forget this loss?

Answer: In HMRC's Property Income manual at www.hmrc.gov.uk/manuals/pimmanual/PIM4210.htm it explains, like you said, that rental losses can only be set against profits from the same rental business. If that rental business ceases, the losses cannot be used. However, if you look at www.hmrc.gov.uk/manuals/pimmanual/PIM2510.htm you can see the rules for cessation of a rental business. For example, if at the time this rental property is sold the taxpayer still owns another property that they are actively trying to rent out then this rental business has not ceased.

124. Individual Or Collectively Taxed?

Question: I am currently renting my property. We have two bedrooms for rent; to make managing them easier we have separate listings for each bedroom. Therefore, the rooms are separately listed on two different accounts (my wife has one, and so do I) which are managed separately with the money going into different accounts. How will we be taxed? I understand that any rental income below £4,000 is not taxed. As the money is going into separate accounts will HMRC collectively tax us or individually tax us?

Answer: You are referring to the rent-a-room scheme. If you look at HMRC's Property Income manual at www.hmrc.gov.uk/manuals/pimmanual/PIM4010.htm you can see that you and your wife have a limit of £4,250 between you; it is not £4,250 each. But even without the rent-a-room scheme, HMRC treat any rental income from a jointly owned husband and wife rental property as being received 50:50. See www.hmrc.gov.uk/manuals/tsemmanual/TSEM9814.htm.

As from April 2016 the rent a room threshold is £7,500.

125. Is There A Requirement To Declare?

Question: If I set up a property company and have the rent paid directly into the company and don't have the rental money paid to me directly, do I still have to personally declare this rental income held in the company in my self-assessment form for the year the rent money is paid into the company?

Answer: If you are the legal landlord, and therefore legally entitled to the rental income, it won't help to divert the rental income to a company, you will still be taxable on it. However, if you rent out the property to the company and allow the company to sublet the property to a third party tenant, then the rent paid by the tenant to the company will only be assessable on the company. The advantage of this arrangement is that you can charge your company a small rent, perhaps equal to your expenses, and your company can charge the tenant the commercial rent (a much higher figure), so that the real profit is made in the company.

126. How Do We Formalise Future Profits Agreement?

Question: Our situation is that we purchased a flat as a home for our son, thus both listed on the Land Registry and Mortgage Loan. Our son has subsequently moved abroad and the flat has been let under permission to let. The flat is managed by a letting agency who pay income into our son's bank account and from which the mortgage payments are made. We gain no share of profits. We are seeking to reallocate future profits from the default 50:50 to (say) 90:10 in favour of our son (our son having the lower income tax liability). Please advise how this is best formalised and if this has to be notified to HMRC.

Answer: Draw up a written agreement between yourself and son saying that even though the flat is owned 50:50 nevertheless the entitlement to the rental income is going to be in the proportion 90:10, and is actually going to be received 90:10. Then make sure that 90% of the rental income goes into a bank account in his sole name. This agreement does not need to be notified to HMRC unless they question you.

127. What Can A Landlord Charge?

Question: What charge can I, as a landlord, make in terms of calculating for work I've done such as painting instead of employing a painter?

Answer: Unfortunately, it says on www.hmrc.gov.uk/manuals/pimmanual/PIM2080.htm: "A landlord can't deduct anything for the time they spend themselves working in their own rental business" (it says something similar regarding capital expenditure at www.hmrc.gov.uk/manuals/cgmanual/CG15210.htm). A deduction can, of course, be made for the expense of materials purchased.

128. If I Transfer To My Wife Will There Be No Tax To Pay?

Question: I own outright a flat that I let. It generates £595 per month income. I'm a 40% taxpayer and have been declaring the income on my tax return and I guess have been paying tax at 40% on this income. My wife doesn't work. Should I transfer the property into her name? She would then, I presume, pay 0% tax on income up to around £10,000?

Answer: If you have a good marriage and therefore trust your wife, then transferring the property to your wife is a very good idea from a tax perspective, because if she has no other income she will pay no income tax on the £7,140 (12 x £595) annual rental income. However, if you have a mortgage on this property and you are claiming relief on the interest payments against your rental income, then the mortgage will have to be in her name for her to claim the relief.

129. Do I Claim Running Expenses Monthly or Yearly?

Question: I'm thinking of renting my house and am looking at tax issues. With regard to running expenses, can I claim these monthly or yearly? I know I have to do a tax return once a year, is it the same for claiming expenses?

Answer: The tax year for property rental runs from 6 April to 5 April. You need to put together all the rental income in this period, and all the allowable expenses in this period, and put the figures once a year on the self-assessment supplementary pages for UK property. See www.gov.uk/government/publications/self-assessment-uk-property-sa105. See www.hmrc.gov.uk/manuals/pimmanual/PIM1101.htm, which explains the dates that rental income is taxable, and the dates that rental expenses can be offset against rental income.

130.   What Would Be The Tax On The Rental Income?

Questions: When the kids leave home we were thinking of converting it into two flats one for us and one either for them or us to rent out. We just wondered what the tax would be on the rental income if we did this and would it be best to share the utilities or have separate ones.

Answer: I assume that at present you own the whole house. Therefore if you split it into two flats and rent out one flat, you will receive the rental income, and pay tax on it. If you made your (over 18) children partial owners of the rental flat, then you could divert the rental income to them, per www.hmrc.gov.uk/manuals/pimmanual/PIM1030.htm. It requires: (a) a written agreement between you and them before you start diverting to them; and (b) their portion of the rental income actually goes into a bank account in their name. It is best to have separate utility accounts.

131.   What Would Be My Tax Position?

Question: I am thinking of letting out my house as a self-catering holiday property, and moving to the country. What tax would I have to pay on the income? Can I claim back any work needing doing to the property against the tax?

Answer: You will have to pay income tax on the net rental income, i.e. the gross rental income (actually received from the tenant) less the allowable expenses. Unfortunately, allowable expenses do not include the time the landlord himself spends working on the rental properties, only the money he actually pays to other people to work on the rental properties, or the money he actually pays for materials etc. (see www.hmrc.gov.uk/manuals/pimmanual/PIM2080.htm).

132.   Are These Tax Deductible?

Question: I rent out a house which has carpets, curtains, a washing machine and fridge. Is the cost of replacing these tax deductible?

Answer: Currently, the short answer to that question is no. The Government withdrew the 'renewals basis' capital allowance for furnishings in a rental property from April 2013 www.hmrc.gov.uk/manuals/pimmanual/PIM3230.htm. So currently, only the 10% wear and tear allowance for a fully furnished rental property is available. However, the Government announced in the summer 2015 Budget that, as from April 2016, the 10% allowance will stop, and instead there will be a new 'replacement allowance'.

133.   Can I Claim Back Pre-letting Costs?

Question: I am thinking of letting out my house as a self-catering holiday property and moving to the country. What tax would I have to pay on the income? Can I claim back any work needing doing to the property against the tax?

Answer: The simple answer is that income tax would apply to your net rental income. If the conditions of your scenario comply with the furnished holiday lettings rules (see www.gov.uk/government/uploads/system/uploads/attachment_data/file/323821/hs253.pdf), then slightly different income tax rules apply. If the property is currently in a fit state to rent out, and any refurbishment work you do is not an improvement (see www.hmrc.gov.uk/manuals/pimmanual/PIM2020.htm), then the cost can be offset against the rental income.

134.   How Do We Express Our Tax Wishes?

Question: Our house in multiple occupation (HMO) is going to incur large losses in the first year, and these can be claimed back through sideways loss relief. We have been told that my husband can claim solely for this (he is a higher rate taxpayer) and rental income going forward can be in my name only (I pay basic rate). We have also been told we do not need to complete a declaration of trust, as we can just write a letter to each other expressing our wishes. This seems too easy!

Answer: If I understand you correctly, your husband is claiming all the losses sideways (see www.hmrc.gov.uk/manuals/pimmanual/PIM4220.htm) because he is currently the sole owner of the HMO. The intention is that all future rental income profits will be yours only; this can only be if he transfers 100% of the beneficial ownership of the property to you. In order to do this, you will need a written declaration of trust – (see http://www.hmrc.gov.uk/manuals/tsemmanual/TSEM9520.htm).

135.   Will We Have To Pay The 'New Tax'?

Question: I'm a higher rate taxpayer and so am concerned about purchasing a buy-to-let property with the new tax laws about to start. If I bought a flat with my retired father and gave all the rental income to him each month (from the tenants direct to his bank account) would we have to pay the new tax?

Answer: There is no new tax starting in 2017. What is happening is that relief for interest payments is being restricted. If you do not need to borrow to buy the property, or if you do need to borrow, but you are a basic rate taxpayer, then the new rules will not affect you. If you do personally need to borrow and you are a higher rate taxpayer, it will not help you to simply give all the rental income to your father. Some more detailed tax advice would be necessary, beyond the scope of the present column.

136.   Do I Pay Tax At 40%?

Question: I've bought a house and I own my current one outright and will be putting that to rent. If I borrow £20,000 from my parents to 'do up' the new property that I am moving into, can I pay them back by placing them as the persons collecting the rent - i.e. it goes from the letting/managing agent directly into their bank account for 20 months so that the loan is paid off? I'm guessing that is fine in principle, but the question is - do I pay tax at 40% (I am a higher rate earner) or should my parents pay tax at the rate relevant to them? They are both retired and so would pay less tax than me, making the money work better.

Answer: The answer is that you have to declare all the rental income in your own name, and pay tax on it at 40%. Since you own the house, and they don't, the rental income is entirely yours. The £20,000 (or £1,000 per month) that is going directly into their bank account is simply a payment from you to them, to repay the loan.

137.   Will HMRC Penalise Us?

Question: My partner and I own two properties 50:50. We live in both properties and have never rented them out or used either to generate an income. We have just found out now that we should have registered one of them as our main residence. If we do this now, would we be penalised by HMRC?

Answer: Look at www.hmrc.gov.uk/manuals/cgmanual/CG64545.htm, where you can see that if the taxpayer did not make a valid election, then it is a matter of fact which property is the main residence for tax purposes. There is a list of criteria there to determine which house 'deserves' to get the relief. For example: (a) where does the taxpayer spend most of their time? (b) where is the taxpayer registered to vote, etc.?

138. What Would Be Our Best Tax Position?

Question: We have two flats in London, converted from a terraced house. We bought upstairs in July 1982, and lived there until July 2001 as our only residence. It was then renovated and let, but there have been long void periods. It was recently redecorated and is now let. In June 2011, we bought the downstairs flat for £425,000, already tenanted but who has recently left. The flats are worth about £700,000-£750,000 each. Downstairs needs complete renovation before it can be re-let. The decision we need to make is either: (a) to renovate and re-let now; (b) sell both flats separately in different years, or together to a developer; or (c) convert the flats back to a house and redevelop ourselves. Recent house sales in the area have been between £2-3 million. We would expect to do this in the next two or three years when we retire and the potential combined effect of capital gains tax and inheritance tax will play a large part in our decision. We are also not clear of the treatment of renovation or future conversion in the tax computation, but clearly inclusion would help mitigate the bill.

Answer: There is a relevant saying: 'Don't let the tax tail wag the commercial dog'. Do what is best for you commercially, and think about tax second. Whatever profit you make you are going to have to pay tax on it, that is unavoidable. You will get a certain amount of capital gains tax principal private residence relief on the upper flat. Obviously, renovation or refurbishment costs are an allowable expense to offset against any profit.

139. How Do I Claim My Allowances?

Question: I am a trustee of a bare trust personal injury compensation account. The trust will be buying two properties to rent. I believe the two options to be either claim all relevant allowances and total them up and deduct from rental income, or add total rental income and deduct a single allowance against tax of £5,000?

Answer: I do not understand your second alternative. Bare trust income is calculated in the same way as for an individual. So you should calculate all relevant allowable expenses, total them up, and deduct them from rental income. If it is truly a bare trust, then the beneficiary's income tax personal allowance will be available when calculating the tax on income.

140. Can My Wife Share The Rental Income?

Question: My wife works part-time and soon going to leave her job and hence become a non-taxpayer. I am a 40% taxpayer through rental income. Can my wife share the rental income up to her personal allowance limit without transferring the property in her name? If I make her my partner in one property, do I have to apply at land registry or does letting HMRC know suffice?

Answer: You have a few options. You can put the property in joint names, but stipulate in writing that she only has, let's say, 5%, or even 0%, of the beneficial ownership of the property (see http://www.hmrc.gov.uk/manuals/tsemmanual/TSEM9848.htm). If you do not submit a Form 17, she will be taxed on 50% of the rental income. You could leave the property solely in your name, but do a declaration of trust transferring a percentage of the beneficial ownership of the property to her (http://www.hmrc.gov.uk/manuals/tsemmanual/TSEM9520.htm). Then she will be taxed according to her percentage of the beneficial ownership. Note that this declaration of trust does not need to be registered at the land registry.

141. Any Pitfalls We Should Be Aware Of?

Question: Our son cannot pay his mortgage and has depression. To help him, we aim to pay off his mortgage and take ownership of his flat but give him, as parents would, a life tenancy if he wants it. What are the pitfalls for us?

Answer: It may be a better idea for you to lend him the money to pay off the mortgage, but at the same time to obtain a first charge on the property (similar to a mortgage company) for the value of the loan. This would avoid any stamp duty land tax, since you are not buying from him. When he gets back on his feet, he can gradually pay the loan back to you.

142.   Is There An Alternative Strategy?

Question: My wife wishes to buy another buy-to-let property with the £150,000 in her pension fund. She realises that 25% can be released in annual increments. Is there an alternative strategy without incurring an income tax liability?

Answer: It is difficult to advise without knowing more about your specific pension scheme. However, it may be worth asking your pension adviser about the possibility of your pension scheme paying you three 'small pots' of lump sums tax free - usually £10,000 each.

143.   What Would Be Our Best Tax Position?

Question: We have two flats in London, converted from a terraced house. We bought upstairs in July 1982, and lived there until July 2001 as our only residence. It was then renovated and let but there have been long void periods. It was recently redecorated and is now let. In June 2011, we bought the downstairs flat for £425,000, already tenanted but who has recently left. The flats are worth about £700,000-750,000 each. Downstairs needs complete renovation before it can be re-let. The decision we need to make is either: (a) to renovate and re-let now; (b) sell both flats separately in different years, or together to a developer; or (c) convert the flats back to a house and redevelop ourselves. Recent house sales in the area have been between £2-3 million. We would expect to do this in the next two or three years when we retire and the potential combined effect of capital gains tax and inheritance tax will play a large part in our decision. We are also not clear of the treatment of renovation or future conversion in the tax computation, but clearly inclusion would help mitigate the bill. What would be our best tax position?

Answer: There is a relevant saying: 'Don't let the tax tail wag the commercial dog'. Do what is best for you commercially, and think about tax second. Whatever profit you make you are going to have to pay tax on it, that is unavoidable. You will get a certain amount of capital gains tax principal private residence relief on the upper flat. Obviously, renovation or refurbishment costs are an allowable expense to offset against any profit.

144.   Can He Gift Me A Percentage Of The Property?

Question: I am helping a friend to buy his flat from the council under the right to buy act - as he has no means to acquire a mortgage and I have the cash to pay for it outright. The idea is to then rent the flat out and the rent will be paid back to me, and I will declare the income myself. Shall I have a solicitor draw a personal mortgage, or can he gift me a percentage of the property, so that I can collect the rent?

Answer: From your perspective you are best off drawing up legal documents showing that you have a charge on the property for the amount of the loan. Additionally you should arrange that you own a small percentage of the property, even 1% will do. Then you can draw up a written agreement between you that even though you only own 1% of the house, nevertheless you will be entitled to and receiving, let's say, 100% of the rental income - see www.hmrc.gov.uk/manuals/pimmanual/PIM1030.htm.

145.   Unfurnished/Furnished – Important Or Not?

Question: I have two queries: I purchased new properties to let unfurnished and they come with integrated appliances within the capital cost: after five years repairing a washing machine it was no longer possible and it needed to be replaced, so I purchased a similar model as a replacement. The cost as I see it is an expense as it is only putting back what was there before. I have not claimed any capital allowances or wear & tear as the property is let unfurnished. My second query is I have a property, it was acquired nearly new and in A1 condition and was let for ten years managed by local agents. The property was not managed well and handed back in an appalling condition resulting in costs of replacing the kitchen, floor coverings and the doubled glazed wooden windows, which were rotten from the inside out. This is not an improvement but given the circumstance a refurbishment costing £15,000 – what is the tax situation please?

Answer: 1. What you describe is very logical, and until recently was allowed, under what was known as the 'renewals basis'. However, the Government cancelled this, and now the only recourse for the landlord of an unfurnished residential property is: (a) turn it into a fully furnished property and claim the 10% wear and tear allowance; or (b) get the tenant to pay extra; or (c) 'absorb' the cost yourself. 2. If all you are doing now with this £15,000 refurbishment is bringing the property back up to its previous standard, and you are continuing to let the property commercially, then this expense is an allowable revenue expense.

As from April 2016 a new replacement allowance has been introduced, similar to the old renewals allowance.

146. Property Refinance Costs – What Is The Tax Position?

Question: How are property refinance costs treated for tax purposes? Specifically, legal fees, search fees and new lender's fees. On the original purchase of course all these costs are not allowable for current income purposes, but form part of any eventual capital gains computation.

Answer: On original purchase legal fees, search fees and other fees relating to the purchase are classified as capital expenditure - see www.hmrc.gov.uk/manuals/pimmanual/PIM2205.htm. But fees relating to obtaining loan finance are allowable revenue expenses - see www.hmrc.gov.uk/manuals/pimmanual/PIM2066.htm. If the refinance simply replaces and stands in the shoes of the original finance, then the refinance fees should also be allowed, like the original.

Capital Gains Tax

147. Any Tax If I Sell My Home?

Question: I have a property which I lived in for three years and then let out for one year. I am now going to sell the property. Will I be liable to pay any tax?

Answer: No. You will not be liable to pay any capital gains tax. This is because the last 18 months of ownership are exempt from tax, and so is the period that the property was your main residence. This means that the first three years of ownership are covered by private residence relief and the last year of ownership are covered by the last 18 month of ownership rule.

Therefore, no tax is due.

148. What Is The Most Amount Of Tax?

Question: Is there a maximum amount of tax that can be paid on the sale of a property? In other words, does one stop paying tax when a certain threshold is breached?

Answer: Tax continues to be paid as long as the profit is taxable. In other words there is no threshold level at which you stop paying tax.

149. Is Letting Relief Restricted To Upper Limit Of £40k?

Question: Is letting relief restricted to upper limit of £40k per property or can each partner claim this figure against their share of gain?

Answer: I have seen that a husband and wife are each allowed letting relief of £40,000 (HMRC Manuals CG 64716, 64738), but I haven't seen that this is available to 'each person who has an ownership interest in the property'. This means that if a husband and wife jointly own a property both can claim up to £40,000 private letting relief.

Don't forget that in order to make use of this relief on disposal of the property it must satisfy the following two conditions:

a) It **must** have been classed your Principle Private Residence (PPR) at some stage when you owned it.

b) It **must** have been let out and tenanted.

150.   Can I Select Any Property As My PPR?

Question: I currently live with my parents and have purchased two investment properties that are currently rented out. Am I able to nominate one of the let properties as my principle private residence to benefit from the PPR relief?

Answer: PPR is only available to the owner of a house if he occupied it as his only or main residence. An intention to occupy it is not sufficient.

It is not necessary to have lived in it as the only or main residence for all the period of ownership, but for at least part of the period of ownership it must have been the only or main residence.

The HMRC say in IR Interpretation 73 that "it is the quality of occupation rather than the length of occupation which determines whether a dwelling-house is its owner's residence".

151.   Can I Claim Private Letting Relief?

Question: I have a property that I have been letting out for the past four years, ever since I purchased it. Can I claim private letting relief even if I have not lived in the property?

Answer: It is important to understand that private letting relief can only be claimed if a property has both been let out and also been lived in.

Therefore, as the situation currently stands, you will not be able to claim private letting relief. However, if you make the property your primary residence then you will be able to claim the relief.

152.   Can I Offset Costs If I Have Lived In The Property?

Question: When the first part of property ownership is claimed as residential ownership (i.e. I live in the property) can:

a)   purchase costs of the property be claimed as relief
b)   refurbishment costs, carried out during the residential period, be claimed as relief

… when I decide to sell the property?

Answer: The simple answer to this question is yes - both purchase costs and major refurbishment costs can be added to the acquisition costs of the property, to set off against the sale proceeds, to reduce the capital gain when the property is disposed of.

Case Study:

Louise buys her first home in August 1998 for £50,000. The purchasing costs are £700 and include solicitor's fees, survey fees etc.

In May 1991 she has a conservatory built. The cost of this is £15,000.

In June 1995, she moves in with her long-term boyfriend and rents her property out.

She finally decides to sell her first home in June 2014, she is able to claim relief on the £700 purchasing costs and the cost of the conservatory against the capital gain.

153.   Can I Sell My Property Below Market Value

Question: My house (my only property) is perhaps valued at £190,000. Can I sell it to my daughter (a single parent) for less than this?

Answer: You can sell your house to your daughter for whatever figure you want. However for tax purposes it is deemed that you sold it to her for its present market value – the figure it would fetch on the open market in an arm's length sale to a third party. For tax purposes this is the figure for which you are deemed to sell it, and it is also the figure your daughter is deemed to buy it for. In your case it would appear to be £190,000. If this house is your principal private residence then the sale should not trigger any capital gains tax liability for you. This can be seen on page http://www.hmrc.gov.uk/manuals/cgmanual/CG14530.htm of the HMRC Capital Gains Manual.

154. How Can I Make Sure I Pay Minimal Capital Gains Tax?

Question: I live with my wife and the house is in her name. In the meantime, I have bought two residential houses in my name, not with buy-to-let-mortgages, and have rented them out. The houses were bought from an investment point of view. I bought one house nearly three and a half years ago and the other house one and a half years ago. I don't mind changing to buy to let mortgages, but before I do that I want to make sure that I should be paying minimal capital gains tax when I sell. How can I do that? We are both in the higher tax paying group.

Answer: From what you described in your question, it would be a good idea to make your wife a joint owner a short time before you plan to sell a property. That way you will have the advantage of her capital gains tax annual exemption to reduce the gain on sale. This will save tax on that amount at 28%. If you have children and you don't mind giving them a bit of the property, you could give them a small portion of the property up to an amount that you don't pay any capital gains tax on the transfer, i.e. so that the gain on the transfer is equal to your annual exemption. Then, when you eventually sell the property, you can utilise their annual exemption(s) as well.

155. When Should We Gift Our Son a Property We Are Buying?

Question: We are currently looking to buy a property for cash which we will then rent out. We would like this to be for our son who will soon be 17. Is there any way we can do this at the time of purchase?

Answer: Since your son is under 18 he cannot legally own property. So you can purchase the property in your names as the legal owners (bare trustees or nominees), so that your names will be on the official documents, and instruct the solicitor to draw up a deed of trust at the time of purchase explaining that your son has the beneficial ownership of the property. When he becomes 18 it is a simple procedure to transfer the legal ownership to him.

156. What Are The Tax Implications, If Any, of Selling Part of My Garden?

Question: I am currently discussing selling part of the garden of our only residential property and would like to know if tax is payable on the proceeds. The land would probably be sold to a builder for the construction of two semi-detached houses.

Answer: The capital gains tax exemption for principal private residence includes grounds not exceeding half a hectare (approximately 1 1/4 acres), or such larger area as is appropriate to the size and character of the house. If some of the land is sold, including for the purpose of building plots, the sale is covered by the exemption so long as the land was enjoyed as part of the garden and grounds, and is sold before the house is sold or at the same time the house is sold (but not after the house is sold).

157. Do I Have To Live In It To Be Exempt From Tax?

Question: If I bought a plot of land and built a house, would I pay tax if I sold it and used all the sale proceeds to purchase another property or land, or would I have to live in it firstly as my principal private residence (PPR)? If I move in, how long do I have to live there for exemption?

Answer: If you sell the house without living in it - yes, you will be liable to tax. If you live in it before you sell it - you can make it into your PPR. There is no fixed answer to how long you need to live in it to make it your PPR. You need to be able to demonstrate that you moved in with the intention to stay long term. Some tax advisers would say you need to live in it for at least between six months and a year.

158. Do I Qualify For Principal Private Residence Relief?

Question: I've lived in freehold house for a number of years, and have now performed a 'sale and leaseback' to an LLP of which I am the main member. I will not live in the house any longer. When I sell the leasehold interest, will I still get principal private residence (PPR) relief for the years lived in the house and the final 18 months? My interest in the house is now leasehold as opposed to freehold, but it is the same house.

Answer: Firstly see www.hmrc.gov.uk/manuals/bimmanual/BIM82115.htm, where you can see that, for tax purposes, an LLP is transparent, so it is considered as though you personally still own the freehold, or possibly a proportion of it that corresponds to your interest in the LLP. Also see www.hmrc.gov.uk/manuals/cgmanual/CG64600.htm, where you can see that PPR relief is available on a disposal of an interest in a dwelling house, and that includes a leasehold interest. Also look at www.hmrc.gov.uk/manuals/cgmanual/CG64930.htm where you can see that where a taxpayer has held different interests at different times, the period of ownership begins at the first date on which expenditure is incurred which would have been deductible in computing any capital gain.

159. Acceptable Or Not?

Question: Is gifting my son a share of my second home to avoid capital gains tax acceptable to HMRC?

Answer: I am afraid not. Any gift to a connected person (e.g. a son) is treated like a sale at market value. See www.hmrc.gov.uk/manuals/cgmanual/CG14530.htm. So even though you may receive no money from your son, HMRC will treat the transfer as though you did, and you will have to pay capital gains tax.

160. Do I Have More Than One PPR?

Question: I am aged 78 and a retired builder with a property with a garden, in total under 0.5 hectares. I lived in this house for 5 years around 11 years ago, and whilst living in it got planning permission to build two houses in the garden. I sold off the two plots for £120,000 and £150,000 respectively and kept the house as a holiday home. With the proceeds of the two plots sold I then bought another property which I have lived in for the past 6 years. I want to go back to living in the house which is now the holiday home and sell the one I am in now. Please can you tell me my PPR position?

Answer: See www.hmrc.gov.uk/manuals/cgmanual/CG64545.htm where it is explained that, when the taxpayer does not make an election, his PPR is a matter of fact - i.e. where he lived as his main home determines which of his two houses is his PPR. So for the first 5 years the original house (A) was your PPR, and then when you moved into the new house (B), B became your PPR for those 6 years. If you now move back to A, A will become your PPR again and B will stop being your PPR. A taxpayer cannot have two PPRs concurrently, except for the last 36-month rule, which allows a taxpayer to claim PPR relief for the last 36 months ownership of a property, even though he is living in a different property as his PPR during those 36 months.

As from April 2014 the last 36-month rule has been shortened to 18 months.

161. Being Eligible For Private Residence Relief

Question: Do you need to live in the property immediately after purchasing to get the principle private residence relief, or can you rent it out and then move into it at a later date and still get the same relief?

Answer: You do not need to live in the property as soon as you purchased it in order to claim the relief. You can live in the property anytime during the ownership.

162. How Long In A Property Before I Get PPR?

Question: What is the minimum amount of time you need to live in a property before you can claim 'Private Residence Relief'? I have heard it is 6 months, is this true?

Answer: The HMRC has not given any specific guidance as to how long you need to live in a property before you can claim the relief. However, as a general rule of thumb, you should look to make it your **permanent residence** for at least 1 year, i.e. 12 months (but it can be less and there have been successful cases for much less than this). The longer you live in a property the better chance you have of claiming the relief. The HMRC is not necessarily interested in how long you lived in the property. They are more interested in whether the property really was your home!

If you want to claim this relief then here are some pointers that will help you to convince the taxman that a property genuinely was your private residence.

a) Have utility bills in your own name at the property address.

b) Make the property address your voting address on the electoral register.

c) Be able to demonstrate that you bought furniture and furnishings for the property. Keep receipts and prove that bulky furniture was delivered to the property address under your name.

d) Have all bank statements delivered to the property address.

163. How Would CGT Be Applied?

Question: I am looking to acquire a few buy-to-let properties. In order to reduce the capital gains tax (CGT) liability in the future when selling any of these properties, I am planning to draw up a deed of trust with myself and my two sons holding the properties in equal shares as tenants in common. I will be providing the deposits and the mortgages will be in my sole name and the property will be registered in my sole name. Each of us will participate in self-managing the properties and each of us will share any net rental income. With such a trust in place will any future capital gain (on sale) be reduced by three times the annual CGT allowance (i.e. one allowance for each tenant-in- common) before CGT is applied?

Answer: That is correct. Even though the properties are in your name only, as the beneficial ownership of each property is split three ways, the capital gain will be divided amongst the three of you. This is because capital gains follows the beneficial ownership, not the legal ownership. See www.hmrc.gov.uk/manuals/cgmanual/CG70230.htm and www.hmrc.gov.uk/manuals/cgmanual/CG11730.htm.

164. Can I Defer Capital Gains Tax?

Question: I am about to sell a buy-to-let property that has made a £40,000 gain. But I am looking to re-invest this money back into another two more properties. Because I have re-invested the money can I defer paying any tax that is due on the £40,000 profit?

Answer: This is a very commonly asked question and one which is often misunderstood by too many people. Once you have disposed of the buy-to-let property then you are liable to pay capital gains tax. This is regardless of whether you have re-invested the profits or spent the money.

There are only two exceptions to this. One is 'Furnished Holiday Lets'. The other is if the property is the subject of compulsory purchase (or compulsory acquisition by a lessee).

165. What CGT Liability For Property That Is Partly PPR?

Question: Please could you tell me what capital gains tax (CGT) each party would pay if there was a 50/50 ownership at sale, but it was one of the owner's primary residence?

Answer: If A and B own a property 50:50, then the sale proceeds and the base cost of the property are divided in two, and two separate CGT calculations are made, one for A and one for B. If it is A's principle private residence, then A will be exempt from any CGT, but B will be liable in the normal way on B's half. This kind of scenario can occur in a divorce situation, when A stays in the property, and B moves out.

Sometime later the property is sold, but since moving out it is no longer B's PPR. The last three years of ownership of B will be deemed to be occupied and therefore eligible for PPR relief, because previously B actually occupied the property.

166. Can I Avoid CGT By Moving Funds?

Question: I am a sole trader with friends in the Isle of Man. Is it possible to sell a property in the UK and send the proceeds to the Isle of Man, thereby side-stepping CGT, and are there any advantages?

Answer: Assuming that you are UK resident, it is not possible to sell a property in the UK and send the proceeds to the Isle of Man in order to side step UK CGT. If you are determined to avoid UK CGT you will have to become non-UK resident for five full consecutive tax years.

167. Can I Increase Borrowing To Minimise Or Avoid CGT?

Question: I have a house for sale for £115,000. At present I owe £75,000 on it. If I increase the borrowing on it tomorrow to £105,000, then sell it for £115,000 in 8 weeks' time, will I have to pay tax on the £10,000 profit? I do not live in the property.

Answer: The CGT liability is based on the purchase and selling price of the property not on the amount that is owed on the property. For CGT purposes it does not matter what the outstanding finance is on the property. Therefore, if you purchased your property for £50,000 and sold it for £115,000 then you could be liable to pay tax at 18% or 28% on the £65,000 profit. This is even if you owe £115,000 on the property.

168.   Do I Pay CGT If I Build Apartments In My Residence?

Question: I am planning to extend my property (principle private residence) to build two apartments. While I would continue to live in my current property, I want to sell the two new apartments. Do I have to pay any tax from the gains? If yes, then how can it be reduced?

Answer: If the new apartments are essentially separate from the original dwelling with their own entrances, for tax purposes they will be considered separately. Therefore, they will not benefit from principal private residence relief except on the land on which they are built. This assumes that the land was used until now for the enjoyment of the taxpayers dwelling.

So tax will have to be paid on the profit on the apartments.

From your message it seems as though you are doing this as a property development project, not with the intention of keeping long term. If so, the profit will be subject to income tax like any trading income.

If you are a basic rate taxpayer and can take dividends from a limited company without further tax, it may be worth exploring the possibility of doing the project through a limited company.

169.   Will I Be Able To Avoid CGT By Helping My Brother?

Question: I purchased a house for my bankrupt and penniless Brother-in-law in June 2003. He was then 78 years old and is now 80 years old. I have paid all the bills relating to this house except the bills from the utilities. When he dies, am I exempt Capital Gains Tax on this property, assuming the property has increased in value?

Answer: Unfortunately, you are not exempt from Capital Gains Tax (CGT) when he dies. If you would have put the property into trust when you purchased it and then let your Brother-in-law occupy it, you could have avoided any CGT when he died.

This shows the importance of advanced tax planning!

It may be worth your while speaking to a tax consultant to see whether the application of the 'implied trust rules' are relevant to your situation. In short, the 'implied trust rules' are based on a situation in which person A owns a property and person B lives in it. However, in very special circumstances person A can get PPR despite there not being a trust in place.

As mentioned, this only applies to very special circumstances and professional advice needs to be sought.

170. How Can I Transfer To My Children And Avoid CGT?

Question: We have a second home, which we rent out. We have owned it for 3 years and purchased it for £54,000. It is in joint ownership between my wife and myself. Current Value is approx. £130,000 to £140,000.

It is our intention to either transfer to our 2 children (20 & 24 years old) or sell to them. Which is the most tax efficient way in which this can be done (i.e. not paying any CGT at all?) and when is the best time, as we are in no hurry. Assume that the property has not been PPR at any point.

Answer: Since the property has never been a 'Principle Private Residence' (PPR) at any point, it is purely an investment property. As such, the only relief available to the owners on a gain when it is disposed of, is annual exemption (AE) – currently £11,100.

If it is given to children, it is deemed to be transferred to them at present market value, whether they actually pay this in cash to the parents or whether they pay nothing. This therefore means that the parents will be taxed on a gain of £130K to £140K, less £54K, less AE as above.

If you hold it for a longer period then you could gift the property in stages, using your annual CGT exemption. By using this strategy, you could effectively gift £22,200 of the gain to your children free of tax on an annual basis. Of course, this would mean that you would need to gift for several years and would not be able to use your annual CGT allowance elsewhere during this period.

Alternatively, consideration could be given to legitimately making it your PPR, as this will help to wipe out a large chunk of your CGT liability.

171. Will I Pay Capital Gains Tax Or Income Tax?

Question: My aim is to become a full-time property investor. However, I am currently working and cannot afford to quit my job. Therefore, I have decided to start slowly refurbishing properties in my spare time and then selling them on for a profit.

Will I be liable to pay income tax or capital gains tax on the profits that are generated?

Answer: The work you are involved in here will be classed as a 'property trade' and therefore, you will be liable to pay income tax on any profits generated.

172. Is There CGT Due On A Property Purchased For My Mother?

Question: I purchased a house in 1984 for the sole purpose of my mother to live there rent free. I paid the mortgage and all maintenance bills. My mother paid the utility bills. My mother has now passed away and I intend to sell the house. Am I liable for capital gains tax?

Answer: A property owned on 5 April 1988, that has been continuously occupied rent free by a dependent relative since that date, is exempt from capital gains tax (CGT) when disposed of, by virtue of Taxation of Chargeable Gains Act (TCGA) 1992 section 226. A dependent relative includes a mother who has no husband, and also usually includes a mother over 65.

173. Can I Buy Property For A Child Under The Age Of 18?

Question: We are considering buying a property which will be let. Is there a way to buy this property for a child who is 13? Is it possible to put it in some form of trust for your child in order to decrease the tax burden? For example CGT tax etc.

Answer: A minor under the age of 18 cannot own land or property in the UK, so it would have to be owned in trust by trustees, e.g. parents, for the beneficial ownership of the 13-year-old. Any asset owned by a child under 18 and unmarried, derived from the property of the parents that produces income of more than £100 per year, is taxed on the parents as the parent's income.

However, this doesn't apply for CGT purposes.

One possible solution is to create a 'bare' trust. A 'Bare' trust can be created where the child is the beneficial owner, and the parents are the legal owners who hold the property effectively as nominees. When the property is sold it will be taxed only on the child (who will have their own CGT annual exemption and perhaps lower tax bands - if they don't have much other income) and not on the parents.

But it must be remembered that the child cannot be prevented from having the property put into his own legal ownership at age 18.

174. How Will A Cash Back Offer Affect My Future CGT?

Question: I am in the process of buying an off-plan property where I will get a 5% cash back upon completion. The property is being purchased for £200,000, so I will get £10,000 back upon completion. What will be deemed to be the purchase price of the property for CGT purposes?

Answer: HMRC Statement of Practice 4/97 paragraph 35 says that the cash back is not taxable in the hands of the recipient, but it does not deal with the purchase price of the property for CGT purposes.

I have not found anything explicit to answer this question, but from my own understanding, I would say that if the contract states that on completion there will be automatic cash back, then the purchase price for CGT purposes is the net figure, i.e. £190,000 in this case.

175. Can We Save Tax By Buying In Children's Names?

Question: We are in the process of buying a flat for our two children (20 & 24) to live in. We only want to charge them a nominal rent i.e. enough to cover our small mortgage on the property. Does that cause any problems when submitting a tax return and will the property be subject to CGT if we decide to sell?

Answer: If the rental income is completely offset by the interest repayments (not capital repayments) of the mortgage, then you will have nil rental income and will not have any concern with the tax return. However, the property will be subject to capital gains tax when sold because principal private residence relief is not available, since the owners are not the occupiers. There are ways around this involving trusts, but this involves advanced tax planning.

From April 2017 there are going to be new rules for a residential property landlord claiming relief for interest paid to a lender.

176. Should I Incorporate?

Question: I'm starting a property development business with three other people. Our intention is to buy from auction, refurbish and sell at a profit (target 3 per year).

Q1: Will the profits be classed as CG or will it be subject to corporation tax?

Q2: Is it beneficial to incorporate the new company or form a self-employed partnership?

Answer:
Q1. This is a trading activity and therefore not subject to CGT. If you operate through a limited company the profit will be subject to corporation tax without the benefit of indexation relief, and if not through a limited company, then the profits will be 'self-employed' or 'partnership' profits.

Q2. This is a question that almost every single property investor asks at some point. Unfortunately it is not a straightforward answer.

Generally speaking it may be preferable to operate through a limited company. However, I could not give you a proper answer until you told me:

- what other annual income you have,
- what is your marginal rate of tax,
- whether you have controlling shareholding in any (other) companies,
- whether you have a need to withdraw the annual profits out of the company,
- what level of profits the company is likely to make, etc.

177. The Easiest Way To Avoid CGT

Question: What is the easiest way to avoid CGT?

Answer: The easiest ways to avoid CGT is to have a property benefit from private residence relief throughout the entire ownership. If the property is deemed to have been your main residence for the entire ownership period then there is no CGT liability.

178.   Can I Use Remainder Of My CGT Allowance?

Question: I sold a property and used up £3,000 of my annual CGT allowance as there was only a £3,000 profit. Will I now lose the remaining allowance?

Answer: No, you will not lose the remaining part of the allowance as long as it is used within the remainder of the tax year. The Annual CGT allowance must be used within the tax year. There is no need to use it all in one go, but an unused amount cannot be carried forward into the following tax year.

179.   Can I Claim Unused CGT For Previous Years?

Question: I understand that there is a capital gains tax allowance, but I was told that you can claim an allowance for previous years. Is this so, and how does it work?

Answer: You have been misinformed. It is not possible to claim capital gains tax allowances for previous years. You are only able to use the CGT allowance of the current year. If you fail to make use of it and the tax year changes then you can only use the allowance in the current year.

180.   Can I Transfer My CGT Allowance?

Question: My partner has a property in his sole name. Can I transfer my unused CGT allowance to him so he can utilise my allowance as well?

Answer: No this is not possible. Only the people owning the property can use their CGT allowances.

181.   How Can My Partner Reduce CGT?

Question: My Partner and I live together in my house. We are not married and he does not pay any mortgage or bills here. He bought a house close by that he rents out and has never lived in. We now wish to sell his house and for him to move in here on a more permanent basis.

Is it possible for him to move into his house for the time being to limit capital gains tax as he has never lived there, there is no PPR as it stands, he lived away. I had had a very nasty divorce I was not willing for him to be put on this mortgage and advised him to keep a foot on the housing ladder.

Now it seems he is liable for CGT if he sells. Any advice on this would be great!

Answer: This is a frequently asked question. The answer is unfortunately not clear cut. However, it may be fair to say that; a) if your partner has no other property that is eligible to be his PPR because he owns no other residence, nor does he rent any other residence, and; b) he moves into this (until now) investment property with all his belongings 'lock, stock and barrel' and informs every one of his new address, and; c) he stays there and lives there fully for six months to a year, then more than likely the HMRC would accept that this residence is his PPR.

Concerning point a, even if he has another property that is eligible to be his PPR, if he makes an election to the HMRC that the residence that he is moving into now is now his PPR and not the other residence, then it will legitimately become his PPR.

182. What Is The Tax Date For CGT Purposes?

Question: What is the tax date for CGT purposes? Is it the date the contracts are exchanged or the date the completion takes place.

Answer: There is a common misconception that the tax date for a sale of a property is the completion date of a property. This is not true. The tax date for CGT purposes is actually the date the contracts are exchanged.

183. Will I Still Be Liable To Capital Gain Tax?

Question: I have let out my only home for the last 12 years. If I move back into the house, register myself on the electoral roll for 6 months and put it up for sale as the only home that I own, will I still be liable to capital gains as I am selling the house that I live in?

Answer: You are exempt from Capital Gains Tax (CGT) for the period you originally lived in the house. Since it was at one time your main residence, the last 18 months of ownership are also exempt from CGT. The gain attributable to the 12 years that the property was let out can be reduced by the 'letting exemption'. This is the smaller of two figures:

a) £40,000, and

b) the amount exempt due to the period you originally lived in the house and the last eighteen months of ownership.

There is another relief that may or may not be relevant in your case. If someone occupied a house as their main residence, then moved away, and then returned to the house as their main residence, then under certain circumstances the intervening period can be treated as 'deemed occupied'.

However, the rules are intricate and would need a more full explanation than this space allows.

184.   How Can I Avoid Paying CGT?

Question: Three years after the death of our parents, the probate has been finalised and I, along with my two sisters and my two nieces, will jointly own a property worth around £600,000.

At the time of death, the property was valued at £400,000 so if we were to now sell, we would presumably pay CGT on the difference?

I was thinking of moving in to the property myself for a while to avoid paying CGT but how would the rule affect my relatives?

Is there another way around this?

Answer: Your presumption is correct. If you were to sell now, you would have to pay CGT on the difference - £200,000. However, since five people have a portion each in the property, five capital gains tax annual exemptions should be available to reduce the overall capital gains tax on a sale.

If you fully move into the property for long enough, it would become your principal private residence, and reduce the CGT liability - but only on your portion of the property. The remainder of the property, owned by your sisters and nieces, would not be eligible for any relief.

There is not really another way around this (that I know of) and three years after death is too late to do a variation of the will.

Any transfer now between any of the inheritors would be deemed to be at present market value, for capital gains tax purposes.

Attempting to substitute £600,000 for £400,000 as the probate value, even if it could be done, would not benefit your situation, since it would most likely result in more inheritance tax to be paid, at 40%, as opposed to capital gains tax at 18% or 28%.

185. Can I Use The CGT Allowance Twice?

Question: I never used my CGT allowance the previous tax year, but this year I am going to sell a property with a considerable gain. Can I use the unused CGT allowance from last year as well?

Answer: No, this is not possible. Once a tax year has passed then any unused CGT allowance from that year cannot be carried forward.

186. How Do I Work Out Capital Gains Tax (CGT)?

Question: I have two houses, both on buy to let mortgages, and I am thinking of selling one house; can you please tell me about CGT and how is it best to work this out because I have a mortgage on the house.

Answer: CGT is calculated on the difference between the sale proceeds and the acquisition value / price, i.e. how much you get for selling it and how much you paid for it. The fact that you have a mortgage, or how much the mortgage is, is not relevant to CGT in normal circumstances (this is a mistake that many people make - you are in good company!).

The mortgage is relevant to CGT only in a scenario in which the purchaser takes over the mortgage from the seller, as part of the deal. In such circumstances, tax law adds the amount of the mortgage taken over to the amount actually paid by the seller to determine the final selling price. See page CG78600, http://www.hmrc.gov.uk/manuals/cg4manual/CG78600.htm, on HMRC Capital Gains Manual.

187.   When Do I Pay Capital Gains Tax (CGT)?

Question: If I get planning consent and build a house in my garden (we occupy the main house), do I pay CGT when I sell it? If so, can I live in it for a short time to offset the tax?

Answer: Yes, you will be liable to tax if you sell a new house that you build in the garden of your existing home, if you do not occupy it as your principal private residence (PPR). If you sell it soon after completing the building, most likely HMRC will classify you as a property developer and charge you to income tax (and Class 2 & 4 National Insurance contributions) on the profits.

If you rent out the new house for some time, HMRC will most probably accept that the profit you make on the eventual sale should be assessable to CGT, and not Income Tax (and NIC). If, however, you move into the new house for an extended period of time and make it your legitimate qualifying PPR then the profit on sale will escape tax due to PPR relief.

188.   Will I Be Liable for Capital Gains Tax (CGT) On The Income From Let Property?

Question: I am exempt from paying tax on my income as I am a non-UK resident. I will soon be renting out my UK flat which currently has an interest only mortgage on it. If I was to use the extra income gained from the rental to make capital overpayments on that mortgage, will I be liable for CGT even though I'm putting it back to reduce my mortgage?

Answer: There is no liability to CGT unless you sell or give away (dispose of) the property, so that there is a change in the beneficial ownership of the property. When you make capital repayments on a mortgage there is no disposal of the property, so no CGT is triggered. See page CG12700 of the HMRC Capital Gains Manual: http://www.hmrc.gov.uk/manuals/cgmanual/cg12700.htm

189. Will I Just Pay CGT On Market Value If I Sell An Inherited Property?

Question: My husband plans to leave me a BTL property that he owns on his death, which is at present rented by my son. He paid £40,000 for it and the market value is now approximately £120,000. He has been advised that if I live in it there will not be any CGT to pay. My concern is what will then be the CGT liability upon my death? I have been advised that if I sell the property straight away I will only pay CGT on market value less value at time of bequeathment. Is this right?

Answer: When your husband dies and you inherit the property from him then its value at the time of death (probate value) will be your base cost for any subsequent sale by you of the property. There is no CGT on death. So if you keep the property until you die, those who inherit from you will pay no CGT, although they may need to pay inheritance tax. As far as CGT is concerned, therefore, there is no necessity for you to sell the property.

190. How Can We Avoid Capital Gains (CGT)?

Question: We have a small family situation whereby we have a property inside a partnership which needs to be transferred to some form of limited company with different shareholders. Do you have any suggestions on how we can achieve this without being effected by capital gains? We will consider offshore or other structures if this helps as we simply do not have the funds to pay the tax gain.

Answer: Unless you are incorporating a business and the property is used commercially in the business (in which case a form of rollover / holdover relief is available) then I do not really have a good answer for you. Rollover / holdover relief is only available for investment property because of a) compulsory purchase, or b) in a case of furnished holiday lettings.

Furthermore, putting the property into a connected limited company will trigger stamp duty land tax based on the present market value of the property, irrespective of what the limited company pays the present owners for the property. Just for comprehensiveness, I should mention that the tax on the capital gain on any asset can be deferred by reinvesting the gain in an EIS company - but this relief is not so practical to apply in most real life cases.

191. Capital Gains Tax and PPR

Question: I plan to rent my current house and buy another. If it doesn't work out with the renting then I want to sell it in a year or two. Will I still incur capital gains tax (CGT)? How long before the CGT kicks in on the house? Also how do I direct the rent to a lower taxed partner...what's the process and where can I get more information?

Answer: If you have occupied your original house as your main residence for all the period of ownership, until now, then if you move out of it you have three years in which to sell it without incurring any capital gains tax (CGT). If you sell after 3 years you will be liable to CGT on the intervening period between moving out and three years before the sale (i.e. the last three years of ownership are exempt). So to give an example, if you move out in February 12, and sell in November 15, you will be liable to CGT for the period February 12 to November 12. If you rent out your original house after moving out, then you will have a 'letting exemption' to reduce the gain on the intervening period, February 12 to November 12 in our example. Depending on the figures involved, and the length of the intervening period, the letting exemption could reduce this gain to zero.

If your partner is married to you, you will need to transfer part (or all) of the property to them, and you will both be taxed on the rental income according to the underlying ownership of the property. E.g. if you own 65% of the property and they own 35%, you will be taxed on the rental income according to the proportion 65:35 respectively. Additionally HMRC will have to be informed by a declaration on Form 17, and the Form 17 needs to be returned to HMRC within 60 days of completion.

If your partner is not married to you, then as long as both of you own a bit of the property, you can come to a (written) agreement between the two of you that the rental income should be split in whatever proportion you want, in accordance with http://www.hmrc.gov.uk/manuals/pimmanual/PIM1030.htm.

As from April 2014 the last 36-month rule has been shortened to 18 months.

192. If We Sell At A Loss, Will We Still Have to Pay CGT?

Question: We are looking to move and are considering a buy-to-let scheme on our house in order to rent this property out. We purchased the property at £250K and it is currently valued at £230K. If we rent the property out for a year or two and then sell at £230K, will we still have to pay CGT even though the sale was at loss to the original purchase price?

Answer: If you look on HMRC website Capital Gains Manual at page CG14200 (www.hmrc.gov.uk/manuals/cgmanual/cg14200.htm) you can see that the capital gains computation is simply the disposal proceeds less the original expenditure. In your case this results in a negative £20,000 figure so you will have no CGT to pay.

193. CGT Or Corporation Tax or Both?

Question: If I buy a property under a company and sell for a profit what tax do I pay?

Answer: If a limited company buys an investment property or a property used in the business of the company (i.e. a capital asset) and sells it sometime later at a profit, the company has made a capital gain, which is calculated according to the rules of capital gains tax, and the resultant profit/gain is subject to corporation tax.

194. Is There A Capital Gains Risk And/Or An Offset?

Question: Twenty years ago, I inherited a house and some land. I ran cattle on the land as a small-holding until 15 years ago. A neighbour has offered a considerable amount for 1 acre adjacent to their house. I am self-employed earning around £20,000 a year. How do I sit with capital gains tax (CGT) and any potential to offset the gain by buying other land?

Answer: If you would be selling the land at the same time as stopping your business, then maybe entrepreneur's relief would be available to reduce the CGT, due to the 'associated disposal' rules. However since the gap between the two in this case is 15 years, this relief cannot apply - see www.hmrc.gov.uk/manuals/cgmanual/CG64000.htm at the end of *Example 2*. Rolling over the gain by investing in some other land is also not an option in your circumstance - it has been too long since you ceased trading, and rollover relief is not available for investment property.

195. Will This Avoid CGT?

Question: If my husband and I both I gift our daughter part of our buy-to-let (BTL) house each year (and the gift is under our annual CGT allowance) can my husband and I still take all the rental income? We want her to eventually own the BTL house but we're trying to avoid paying CGT on the gift.

Answer: You can draw up a written agreement (preferably before the start of the tax year) that even though the house is owned 90:10 or 80:20 etc., nevertheless the rental income is going all to you and your husband. Thereafter make sure the rental income actually goes to the bank account of you and your husband (I assume your daughter is over 18).

196.   Should I Move Into Previously Rented Out Property?

Question: If I buy a 2nd property and rent it out for a couple of years , is any tax due on it if I then sell my primary residence and move into this 2nd property making it my primary residence for the next 10 years before selling it?

Answer: If you sell your first (primary residence) property and if it has been classed as your main residence then there will be no tax due on this property. If after two years you then move into the previous rented property then you may well have a small CGT liability in the future.

However, a huge chunk of the tax liability will be avoided because you will benefit from private residence relief. However, you will also receive another favourable tax relief i.e. private letting relief.

The latter relief along with your annual CGT allowance could well wipe-out any CGT liability. However, in the case that a CGT liability still remains, it is likely to be nominal when compared with the gain you have made on the property.

197.   Can I Give A Family Member A Financial Gift?

Question: Can I give a family member a financial gift and account for it within my self-assessment returns?

Answer: You can certainly give a family member a financial gift. However you do not account for it on a self-assessment return, unless it is an asset that would be assessable to capital gains tax (CGT) had you disposed of it to a third party.

As far as income tax is concerned, it has no impact. This is because I assume it is a pure gift, and not in return for any work performed.

As far as Inheritance Tax (IHT) is concerned, it is a Potentially Exempt Transfer (PET), and falls out of any IHT calculations if the donor survives for seven years. The HMRC do not need to be informed of PET's during lifetime.

As far as CGT is concerned, if it is a non-cash asset that is worth more at the time of disposal than at the time of acquisition, then it is quite possible that the donor is liable to CGT on the gift, even though he/she receives nothing from the recipient in return for the property.

198. How Do You 'Gift A Property In Stages'?

Question: How do you 'gift a property in stages' to use annual CGT exemptions?

Answer: Gifting a property in stages is the same as gifting a whole property. Your solicitor will draw up the required documents for the conveyance of a percentage of the property and register the transaction with the Land Registry.

In order to calculate what percentage to transfer, you need to look at the present market value of the property, its acquisition cost, any principal private residence and letting relief available, and choose a percentage that reduces the gain to approximately the annual exemption available.

Of course, there are a number of relief's that may be available, for example, principal private residence relief, CGT allowance to help reduce the liability.

199. Avoiding Tax When Splitting A Property

Question: My mother and I have lived in our house for 35 years. I have converted the house into 2 dwellings and intend to have separate leases on them. Will we be liable for CGT at any time? If so, what is the best way to avoid this?

Answer: This question is not very clear so I need to make some assumptions. I assume that the mother owned the whole house until they decided to split the house in two, at which point she transferred ownership of half of it to the child. If so, there will be no capital gains tax liability because principal private residence relief will be available on both halves of the house.

The mother owned the whole house until the split and lived in it. She owned and lived in her half after the split. The child owned and lived in their half after the split. So the conditions for the relief have been complied with and there will be no tax due.

200. Tax Treatment For New And Replacement Kitchens

Question: We recently bought a property for Buy-to-let. It needed a new kitchen before it could be let. We also had to redecorate throughout. Obviously we will have to redecorate again between each tenancy.

Is the cost of original decoration offset against rental income or CGT when we sell? Also, what if we have to put in another new kitchen before reselling? Can we claim the cost of 2 new kitchens against CGT?

Answer: In short the first kitchen replacement would appear to be a capital expense and any subsequent kitchen replacements a revenue expense (i.e. can be offset against the rental income).

According to the HMRC guidelines, I believe that the first new kitchen is a capital expense because the property was unable to be let out until the kitchen was replaced. Also, a new kitchen is likely you have increased the value of a property.

However the subsequent replacement kitchens are just re-instating a worn out or dilapidated asset and are therefore a revenue expense. The redecorating is a revenue expense as the HMRC states that:

Examples of common repairs, which are normally deductible in computing rental business profits, include:

- *exterior and interior painting and decorating;*
- *stone cleaning;*
- *damp and rot treatment;*
- *mending broken windows, doors, furniture and machines such as cookers or lifts;*

- *re-pointing; and*
- *replacing roof slates, flashing and gutters.*

It would seem to me that a property can usually be let out even though it needs redecorating and therefore any costs incurred for re-decorating prior to and during lets can be offset against the rental income.

201. Transferring Property To Your Children

Question: If I give a rented property to my child, what tax does she have to pay now and if she decides to sell it in the future, and on what "purchase" price will she have to pay CGT (original or price at time of gift)?

Answer: If a parent gives a rented property to a child, the property is treated for tax purposes as though it changed hands at present market value, even though the child paid nothing to the parent for it. Therefore, it is quite likely that the parent will be liable to capital gains tax on the transfer, but not the child.

If the child is under 18 and unmarried and the property produces rental income of more than £100 per year, then all the rental income, for tax purposes, is deemed to be the income of the parent and they are taxed on it accordingly.

Otherwise the rental income is attributed to the child and they have a personal allowance to set off against it, like any other taxpayer. If the child decides to sell the property in the future, the acquisition cost they can use to set off against the sale proceeds (in order to calculate the capital gain) will be the value at the time of the gift.

202. What Tax If I Immediately Sell An Inherited Property?

Question: I am a house owner and am about to inherit a 2nd property (worth approx. 150k) which solicitors (executors of the will) are about to put in my name.

If I sell it straight away would I avoid Capital Gains Tax (presumably yes as I will not make more than 8k from the time I get it and actually sell it). My main concern is, as it will be my 2nd property, would I have to pay more/extra CGT or be a victim of another tax/charge?

Answer: When someone dies and passes an asset to an inheritor, the inheritor receives the asset, for tax purposes, at probate value, i.e. market value at the time of death. There is no capital gains tax on death, but there is an uplift, i.e. the recipient receives it at present market value.

203. Using Your CGT Allowance On A New Build

Question: I am planning to resell an off-plan property I have just purchased, but will not be ready until next year. Can my wife and I use our CGT allowance when it is sold?

Answer: The answer to your question depends on what your original intention was.
If you originally intended to sell the property straight after completion, it may be classed as a 'dealing trade' and your profits at the point of sale will be subject to income tax. Therefore, no CGT allowances will be available.

However, if your intention was to let the property, but given the dramatic increase you have now decided to sell, then you can both claim your annual CGT allowances which currently stand at £11,100 for the 2016-2017 tax year.

Remember - The property must be in joint names before both you and your wife can claim the annual CGT allowance.

204. How Is Property Ownership Determined?

Question: My 2 brothers-in-law live in the same house and are joint owners. One of them is getting married and is moving out. When he moves out, will he still retain ownership of his share of the property?

He has suggested that his brother buy him out and is willing to accept about 50% of the value of his share of the property, which is approx. £100k. Are there any tax implications to this move? The property is worth approx. £200k.

Answer: When the brother moves out he will still retain ownership of his share of the property. If the present market value of the property is £200K and he sells 50% of the property (i.e. his share) to his brother (i.e. a connected person) then the HMRC will treat this as a sale for £100K, whether he actually receives £100K from his brother or not.

This figure of £100K is what he will have to use in his capital gains tax (CGT) computation.

If he has lived in the property all the period of ownership, the disposal is exempt from CGT due to principal private residence relief.

However, if the property is a UK residential property, then even though the owner is non UK resident, they will be liable to UK CGT on any increase in value from April 2015 onwards.

205. Can I Transfer My Property?

Question: If I am the landlord of a property with a market value of £300,000 and outstanding mortgage of £60,000. Is there a tax-free way of transferring the property to someone else for £60,000? In effect they would just pick up the outstanding mortgage. Please assume I haven't lived in the property for some years and have lived in the US since 2001. This would help out a cousin who has just lost her husband and has 4 young children.

Answer: Because you are not making an 'arm's length disposal', you are deemed to be disposing of the property at its present market value, i.e. £300,000, even if in actuality you only receive £60,000 for it, or any other sum. Therefore, your capital gain is the difference between £300,000 and the amount you paid for it.

However, if you are now non UK resident in the tax year when you transfer the property, there is no UK capital gains tax to pay until you become UK resident again. Even if/when you become UK resident again, if you have been non UK resident for the 5 complete consecutive tax years previously, there will be no UK CGT to pay.

206. Can My Brother Discount His Share Of Property?

Question: My brother and I bought a property jointly but the deeds are registered solely in his name. Neither of us have used the property as a main residence. The property was rented over the period and all rents were declared. The purchase price for this property was £50,000 and the current market value is £150,000.

Can my brother now sell this property to me below the market value (e.g. £100,000) to reduce the CGT on the sale?

Answer: It is not clear to me whether you have always had beneficial ownership over half the property, since the date of acquisition, or not i.e. did the contribution of half the purchase price make you an owner of half the beneficial ownership of the house, even though your brother was the legal owner, or was the contribution of half the purchase price by you simply a loan by you to your brother?

An important factor in deciding this question is in whose name was the rental income declared to the Revenue. If it was declared only in your brother's name, this shows that your brother had beneficial ownership over the whole property (see Revenue Capital Gains Manual page CG70230.)

207.   Should I Gift or Use a Lease?

Question: I want to give my godson a property I bought for him some ten years ago. I do not want to pay capital gains tax unless I have to. Is it not possible for me to grant him a long lease of say 60 years at a nominal rent and then in a few years' time allow him to extend the lease and then buy the ground rent? The property currently has a value of about £300,000 and was originally purchased for £150,000.

Answer: Your idea is a good one. Unfortunately others have been down this route already. If you look on HMRC Capital Gains Manual page CG70752 (http://www.hmrc.gov.uk/manuals/CGmanual/CG70752.htm) you can see that it says: "A long lease is a lease with over 50 years to run... long leases are treated in the same manner as freeholds".

Furthermore, since this not a 'bargain at arm's length (see their page CG14530 (http://www.hmrc.gov.uk/manuals/cgmanual/CG14530.htm), the market rule will apply and you will be treated as disposing of the property at its 'present market value', irrespective of the amount your godson pays you for it.

If you are really determined to avoid capital gains tax (CGT), you could consider transferring 6% of the property to your godson this tax year, and doing a similar disposal for the next 15 plus years, in a way that the gain triggered each year is less than the CGT annual exemption (currently £10,100).

208.   Is This My Main Residence Or Not?

Question: I bought a flat 11 years ago and rented it out. I lived in it for 9 months before renting it out. I then moved in with my partner and we rented for 11 years. We now want to sell the property. Does this qualify as my main residence? Also we have spent over £20,000 on refurbishments, can this be taken as a deduction against CGT?

Answer: It is questionable whether this qualifies as your main residence. However, if when you moved in 11 years ago you moved in 'lock stock and barrel', and you lived in no other place at the same time, and you intended to stay long term – but after 9 months a 'life event' occurred which forced you to move, then you have a very good argument for saying that for those 9 months it was truly and legitimately your qualifying principal private residence (PPR). Once a property qualifies as a taxpayer's PPR, then the period of occupation (9 months in this case) plus the last three years of ownership are exempt from capital gains tax. Since you rented out the property in the intervening 8 years (11 – 3) you have a letting exemption available to you to reduce the gain attributable to these 8 years. With regards to the £20,000 refurbishment costs, if a) they are truly capital costs – see http://www.hmrc.gov.uk/manuals/pimmanual/PIM2020.htm for the dividing line between capital and revenue costs, and b) they have not been claimed as a revenue expense against your rental income, then they can be claimed as a deduction against CGT.

As from April 2014 the last 36-month rule has been shortened to 18 months.

209.   Tax Implications Of Gifting A Small Percentage Of Property

Question: We are considering renting our jointly-owned BTL property to my daughter and son in law. What are the tax implications of giving them a small percentage (say, 5%) of the property for each year that they stay there?

Answer: There is no stamp duty land tax on a gift, since the recipient pays no consideration. However there could be a capital gains tax (CGT) liability on you, the donors. However the probability is small. Let's say you purchased the property for £200,000, and now (at the time of the gift) it is worth £300,000. You could gift up to 20% of the property, make a gain of £20,000 and still avoid CGT. This is because the property is jointly owned, and every individual has a CGT annual exemption – that is they can incur capital gains of up to £11,100 (currently) each tax year with no CGT to pay. (This means £22,200 for you and your spouse together.)

210. How Do I Gift My Property To My Son?

Question: I would like to gift my buy-to-let property to my son. I still have a £60,000 mortgage remaining on the property and I also own another property which is my main residence. How do I go about gifting the property to my son and what are the tax implications?

Answer: Because your son is considered a 'connected person' to you, and because you are gifting to him, it is deemed, for taxation purposes, that you sold it to him at 'present market value' (PMV), even though he gives you no money at all for it. The PMV is what you could normally expect to get for it if you sold it to a non-related third party on the open market. If the PMV is more than you paid for it, then you will be liable to capital gains tax (CGT) on the difference.

There won't be any stamp duty land tax on the gift because he is not paying you anything for it. In order to reduce your exposure to CGT you could consider transferring only a portion of the property in this tax year, so that the amount of the gain triggered is matched by your CGT annual exemption (currently £11,100), and doing the same thing in the following year and subsequent years.

211. What Tax Will I Pay On A Transferred Property?

Question: A close friend (non-relative) of mine will shortly be transferring three properties across to me at no cost; I will not pay anything for them. She owns the properties outright and there is no debt secured against them. There are personal reasons for this, which are perfectly legitimate i.e. this is not an attempt of falsifying bankruptcy etc. My intention is to rent out two of the properties and sell the third at its current market price of £230,000. Given that I have never lived in this property, I assume I will be liable for CGT. However, I am unsure how to calculate this especially given that I paid £0 for the property.

Answer: If you look at page CG14530 (www.hmrc.gov.uk/manuals/cgmanual/cg14530.htm) of HMRC's Capital Gains Manual, you will see that in certain situations 'market value' is substituted, for taxation purposes, for the consideration that changes hands. The amount that the recipient/purchaser of the asset actually pays the donor/seller is ignored.

212. What Is The Tax Position On Private Residence Transfers?

Question: I bought some land with one house on it in 1987, and my parents lived in it. The land and house were transferred to my parents in 1991 with no capital gains tax (CGT). I built a house in the garden of the original house while still owned and occupied by my parents and the new house has been transferred back to me. Are there any tax liabilities for either my parents or me?

Answer: I am not sure what you mean by 'transferred back to you'. I would have presumed that if you built the house, obviously with your parents' consent, then the house was yours from 'day 1'. If so the only problem is the land underneath the house. If your parents transfer it to you, then it is quite likely that there is no CGT for them to pay, because most probably they used the land before the building began, and such a transfer is therefore eligible for principal private residence relief. If I am wrong, and the new house belonged to your parents from the beginning, then most probably they will be liable to income tax on its transfer to you.

213. What IHT And Possibly CGT Would Be Payable?

Question: My mother who is 89 wants to transfer the ownership of her house to me and my brother, but to remain living in it. This is primarily aimed at reducing inheritance tax when she dies and avoiding having to sell the property to fund her care should she need to go into a home. What are the current inheritance and capital gains tax implications of this? Also, would she have to pay rent and the running costs of the property? The house is worth approximately £400,000.

Answer: From an inheritance tax (IHT) perspective, your mother will not gain anything by gifting to you the house now, since she is intending to continue to live there; it will be a 'gift with reservation (GWR)'. However, if she pays you a commercial rent for the property, and she pays for the running costs of the property, for as long as she continues to live in the property, like any normal tenant, (so it is not a GWR), and she lives for seven years after gifting you and your brother the property, then this will be a successful potentially exempt transfer (PET), and the house will not be included in her estate when she dies. As far as capital gains are concerned, if she has always occupied the property as her main residence for all the period of her ownership, then when she transfers to you and your brother there should be no capital gains tax due to principal private residence relief. As far as 'avoiding having to sell the property to fund her care should she need to go into a home' is concerned, it is not so simple - the authorities may challenge the transfer and seek to effectively ignore it. You need to look into this before you do any transfers.

214.   True Or False?

Question: My girlfriend and I are splitting up after 15 years. We have two properties in joint names. I moved into the flat six months ago. My partner and three children are staying in the family house and I continue to fund this. We have agreed to sign over each property to each other with no money changing hands. There is a rumour even though both properties are in both our names at the moment and we aren't gaining anything different, apart from taking individual names off the individual properties, so we can move forward in life, we might have to pay capital gains tax and stamp duties. Please can you tell me if this is true or false, as there is no way we can afford to pay out on something we already own and live in?

Answer: There is no stamp duty land tax (SDLT) because this falls under the 'partition relief' rules - see www.hmrc.gov.uk/manuals/sdltmanual/SDLTM04030.htm%20and the example following. This is deemed to be for no consideration, so no SDLT tax return required. Regarding capital gains tax (CGT), see www.hmrc.gov.uk/manuals/cgmanual/CG65170.htm that if you meet the conditions there may be no CGT either.

215.   Can I Offset The Cost For Extending The Lease?

Question: I have purchased a property for £95,000 in the year 2000. Afterwards I was living in the property for two years and have gradually renovated the place. I also bought a lease extension to increase the lease from 74 to 164 years. Before letting it out two years after purchasing it, I re-mortgaged and the property was valued £170,000.

When I sell the property, will I be liable for a CGT, even though I increased the value through my renovation? Also, can I offset the cost for the lease extension (£15,000)?

Answer: Firstly, if the property renovations have been of a 'capital nature', i.e. they have increased the value of the property, they can be deducted from the final selling cost.

Secondly, the cost of the lease extension is an allowable expense for CGT purposes – see the HMRC Manuals page CG 71401.

Thirdly, because you lived in the property, principal private residence relief and private letting relief will be available to reduce the gain.

Probably the CGT annual exemption will also be available.

216. Can We Gift Our Buy-to-Let (BTL) Property To Our Children?

Question: My wife and I jointly own a (mortgaged) BTL property. Our children are now 18 and 19. Can we gift 1% of the property to each child (new share of property capital being 49% / 49% / 1% / 1%) and sign an agreement that all rental income + expenses are to be shared 50:50 between the children? As they are at University, their personal allowance should ensure there is no tax to pay and, of course, my wife and I would pay no tax. Also, would there be any stamp duty or other costs in involved in the 'gifting'?

Answer: Each one of you (the father and mother) should gift 1% of the property, one of you to one child and one of you to the other child. There is no stamp duty land tax on this transaction because it is a gift for no consideration. There most probably will not be any capital gains tax (CGT) either, because we are only talking about 1% of the property, and each one of you has an annual exemption for CGT of £11,100.

Then you draw up two written agreements (the first between one parent and one child, and the second between the other parent and the other child), as you made reference to. As can be seen in HMRC Property Income Manual page PIM1030, this works to 'shift' taxable income from one partner in a property partnership, to another partner.

217. Can We Share PPR And Letting Relief Between Us?

Question: I have a property that I purchased in 1996. In 2002, I married but the property remains in my name only. We let out the property in 2008, and now intend to sell. Any letting income has been shared between us, but when we sell, can we also share the PPR and letting relief available?

Answer: If it is correct that the property is still in your name only, and you also own 100% of the beneficial ownership, then I cannot understand why any letting income has been shared between you, since the property totally belongs to you. And when sold, the sale can only be attributed to you, so there can be no sharing of the principal property relief (PPR) or letting relief. However, if you mean that the property is solely in your legal name, but at some stage you transferred some of the beneficial ownership to your spouse by a declaration/deed of trust, then it depends when you did this. If you did this when you were both living in the property as your main residence, then your spouse takes over your PPR history, and is eligible to the same PPR reliefs as you are - see www.hmrc.gov.uk/manuals/cgmanual/CG64950.htm.

218.   Does He Have To Pay Capital Gains Tax?

Question: My mum died in January, so my dad decided to add my name (daughter) and my husband and eldest son whilst taking my mum's name off the deeds. My youngest son was too young to be added to the deeds. My dad has now decided to sell the house as he cannot live there without my mum. A friend has said that we will have to pay capital gains tax. Is this true?

Answer: I presume that when you write that your father added the three of you to the deeds, he actually gave you a quarter of the property each. If so, when the property is actually sold, in theory there could be capital gains tax for you to pay, but in practice this is very unlikely. When your father transferred to you in January, it was deemed to be transferred   to   you   at   its   present   market   value   -   see www.hmrc.gov.uk/manuals/cgmanual/CG14530.htm. Even if it has gone up in value a bit since January, it is unlikely to have gone up more than the capital gains tax annual exemption of £11,100 (2015-16) for each quarter share.

219.   Would I Have To Pay Capital Gains Tax?

Question: I brought my flat in July 2006 and lived there until April 2010 when I moved into my now wife's house. We rented out the flat due to the negative equity on the property. Now as the market has improved it is on the market. We are also buying my wife's parents' house jointly with my sister and brother in law, if I reinvest any profit from my sale into the purchase of my wife's parents house do I need to pay any capital gains tax?

Answer: Unfortunately, in this country there is no rollover/holdover/reinvestment relief for residential investment property except in two not so usual circumstances: (a) qualifying furnished holiday lettings; and (b) compulsory purchase. However, since you lived in the property from 2006 until 2010 and then rented it out, it is quite possible that you may not have much capital gains tax (CGT) to pay, due to a combination of principal private residence relief, lettings exemption and the CGT annual exemption.

220. Which Property Will I Have To Pay Capital Gains On, If Any?

Question: I live with my parents in their house which they own. I have two buy-to-let properties. If I was to sell one or even both of them, would I have to pay capital gains tax (CGT) on both? Is CGT not meant for a second home? In my case, I am not getting the relief an owner-occupier would get for either of my properties.

Answer: I am sorry to tell you that you will have to pay CGT on both buy-to-let properties. HMRC state emphatically that principal private residence relief from CGT only applies to someone who actually occupies the property as his main residence www.hmrc.gov.uk/manuals/cgmanual/CG64427.htm and subsequent pages.

221. Can We Offset?

Question: We are selling a property which is a buy-to-let property. There is no mortgage. We shall receive about £5,000 less than we paid for it in 2008. Can this loss be offset against either our tax or against a capital gain on other properties?

Answer: This is a capital loss that can be offset against any capital gain you make in the current tax year, or in future tax years. The loss must be offset at the earliest available opportunity. There is no limit to how many years you can carry forward the loss (see www.hmrc.gov.uk/manuals/cgmanual/CG15810.htm).

222.   Which Valuation Figure Would Be Used?

Question: I have lived in my home for 12 years and in that time added a whopping extension. I am hoping to build a new home and move into that, while keeping the second home and letting it. I realise there is an 18 month's extension, but my question is what happens after that? Say I paid £200,000 for my house, then spent a further £100,000 (eight years ago) on extending it. The valuation is therefore considerably more than it would be had we not extended, i.e. when we come to sell let's say the value is £600,000, but had we not extended, £450,000. How does this come into effect with capital gains tax (CGT)? As I understand it, we'd be taxed for CGT for the percentage of time we weren't in the property (plus 18 months), so surely that's unfair as the 'profit' (for want of a better word) was made while in occupation (by natural increases plus the extension). Is there any way I could get a valuation now (or in 18 months), and then pay the CGT on the difference (between sale price and valuation) when we come to sell?

Answer: The way it works for capital gains tax is that you take the entire gain (e.g. £600,000 less £200,000 less £100,000 = £300,000) and divide it by all the years of ownership. Let's say you move out today and sell in three years' time, so your years of ownership are 15. Your capital gain per year is £20,000. The first 12 years are exempt, as are the last 18 months of ownership. So you are only taxable on the 18 months starting today, which equates to a capital gain of £30,000. If you let out the house during this 18-month period you are eligible for the letting exemption, to reduce the £30,000. Unfortunately, the rules do not agree with your suggested method of calculation.

223.   Will There Be A Capital Gains Tax Liability?

Question: If we sell one rental property and, after paying off the mortgage, use the balance to repay the loan on another rental property (which we will keep for the moment) would that balance be liable for capital gains tax (CGT) since it is reinvesting in the same business?

Answer: Not just that balance, but the difference between the sale proceeds and what you paid for that property will all be liable to CGT. Even though you are reinvesting in the same business, unfortunately in this country there is no holdover/rollover or reinvestment relief for a capital gain on a residential investment property except for: (a) compulsory purchase; (b) furnished holiday lettings; or (c) under the enterprise investment scheme rules, which are not compatible with investment in residential property.

224. Does The Age-Related Tax Relief Come Off Capital Gains Tax?

Question: As a non-domiciled UK resident and being over 70, I will be selling a property this year that I have rented out for the past nine years. I have paid tax on the income. What are the capital gains tax (CGT) implications when I sell? Does the age-related tax relief come off the CGT?

Answer: Assuming that the property is in the UK, you will be liable to UK CGT when you sell the property, because you are UK resident. You mention the 'age related tax relief'. I assume that you mean the increased income tax personal allowance because you are over 70. This will not affect the CGT you have to pay. First, you deduct the CGT annual exemption (currently £11,100) from the gain. Any remaining gain falling within the unused basic rate income tax band is taxed at 18%. Any remaining gain after this is taxed at 28%.

225. Conversion Of Main Residence: What Tax Would I Pay?

Question: What are the tax implications of converting a single main residence into two separate dwellings to sell off?

Answer: If you look at:
www.hmrc.gov.uk/manuals/cgmanual/CG65265.htm%20and%20pages%20CG65270%20and%20CG65271, you can see that any gain until the time you start your building work is exempt - due to principal private residence relief (you mentioned that it is a main residence). But the increase in value of the whole property from that point onwards is taxable. From those pages, it appears that the increase is subject to capital gains tax.

226. Sale Of Property: What Are Our Tax Positions?

Question: I have sold a second property in my name and have a gain of £70,000. Can I transfer some of this gain to my wife even though I have realised the gain already, as opposed to transferring part of the asset and then she sells and uses her allowance?

Answer: Unfortunately, at this stage it is too late to reduce your taxable capital gain by simply transferring to your wife. The correct procedure would have been, as you wrote, to have transferred part of the property before the sale to your wife, and then sold, using her allowance.

227.   How Much Of The Repair Etc. Costs Can I Reclaim?

Question: As a landlord, I have let a property to the same couple for the past eight years. Unfortunately, we had to evict them to gain access to the property. They left the property in a very poor state of repair and maintenance and we have had to: (a) spend significant time and effort removing abandoned goods and rubbish from the property which has meant several visits to the property 100 miles from our home incurring overnight stops, travel & accommodation costs; (b) get contractors to do an in-depth clean; (c) get the decorators to do a significant amount of re-decoration; and (d) spend more days working on the garden which had become a wilderness which has incurred more travel and accommodation costs. When this is all done, we plan to sell. How much of the above costs can I reclaim against the potential capital gain of the sale?

Answer: If you look at www.hmrc.gov.uk/manuals/pimmanual/PIM2020.htm, in the section headed 'Dilapidations' (first bullet point), the implication is that your expenditure is not an allowable revenue expense, because it is not in order to further your future rental business; the reason being because your intention now is to sell the property.

228.   Will I Pay Capital Gains Tax?

Question: My husband and I jointly own a property in London, bought around 1995 for £95,000. He recently passed away, and I am now considering selling it. We are Asian but both hold UK passports. We have been ordinarily residing in Asia, but kept the property as our only residence whenever we spent time in London. Do I have to pay capital gains tax when I sell it?

Answer: If you are non-UK tax resident, you are not liable to UK capital gains tax (CGT) on any gains on a UK residential property until April 2015. However, you are broadly liable to UK CGT on any increase in value from April 2015 until the date of sale. I advise you to look at http://www.gov.uk/government/publications/capital-gains-tax-for-non-uk-residents-sales-and-disposals-of-uk-residential-property. It is not easy to determine that you are truly non-UK resident - you would need to look through HMRC's guidance (RDR3), or ask a tax adviser.

229.   When Does Capital Gains Tax Kick In?

Question: How long do I have to live in my new build to avoid paying capital gains tax?

Answer: There is no statutory minimum time period. HMRC say it is not the quantity of the residence, but the quality. You have to move in with the intention to stay long term. So if you ask several tax advisers, you may get a different answer from each one. Having said that, maybe an appropriate answer would be six months to a year.

230.   How Do I Calculate My Capital Gains Tax?

Question: I have a property which was bought in 2002 for £88,000. I bought another property in 2011, and let the first property. So in total out of the 13 years of ownership it was lived in as my primary residence for nine years. The property has been re-mortgaged. The current value of the property is £190,000 and the outstanding mortgage is £101,000. I'm unsure how to calculate roughly how much tax I will have to pay when I sell this house later this year.

Answer: Assuming you sell the house in 2016 ('later this year') for £190,000, having owned it for 14 years, and making a capital gain of £190,000 - £88,000 = £102,000, your gain per year will be £7,286. The first nine years are exempt under the private residence relief rules, due to actual occupation. The last 18 months of ownership are exempt due to the final period exemption. So only the middle 3.5 years are taxable. The capital gain attributable to these years is 3.5 * £7,286 = £25,500. However, since you let the property during those years, the 'letting exemption' is available to you, and it reduces your taxable gain to nil. So no capital gains tax to pay.

231.   Capital Gains Tax – How Can I Reduce This?

Question: Over the last eight years my buy-to-let house value has gone from £120,000 to £220,000. As I understand it, if I sell it now I would be expected to pay capital gains tax (CGT) on the £100,000 profit. Is this correct, or am I allowed some increase over the years? Also, could I sell the house and use the money to buy another as an expense using the £100,000, reducing the amount of CGT to pay?

Answer: When you say 'allowed to have some increase over the years' you are probably referring to some sort of indexation allowance. Unfortunately, this ceased for individuals some years ago. Also, your idea about buying another house and thereby reducing the CGT on the first house is not possible. 'Rollover' or 'holdover' relief from CGT is not available for investment properties except for furnished holiday lettings, or compulsory purchase.

232.   What's The Most Efficient Way To Manage This?

Question: My wife and I have recently bought a small property with our savings. We intend to let it out, but first it requires some work (kitchen, bathroom, complete decoration, etc.). For some work, like roof repairs and electrical works I will pay professionals, and offset that against expenses. Most of the other work I will carry out myself. I've planned for it to take me four months. I'm currently unemployed, hence the project. I would like to know whether, if I'm drawing on savings to support us and pay the home bills, could this be seen as income; would I end up paying basic rate, or can I offset it against capital gains when and if we decide to sell? I just wondered the most efficient way to manage this.

Answer: Firstly, drawing on savings is not considered income, so there is no tax liability on such withdrawals. Secondly, your own labour on your own investment asset is also not considered income. Thirdly, your own labour is not an allowable expense, both for rental income tax purposes (see www.hmrc.gov.uk/manuals/pimmanual/PIM2080.htm) and also for capital gains tax purposes (see www.hmrc.gov.uk/manuals/cgmanual/CG15210.htm)).

233.   Do I Pay Tax On What I Won't Receive?

Question: I'm from Spain, originally, and my parents own a house there. I live in the UK permanently now and am UK tax resident. After my mother's passing, I inherited one-sixth of the house, but that value was never transferred to me - the house was to remain my father's. He is now planning to sell the property to buy a smaller apartment. Will I need to pay tax on my share of the money, even though again - I will not receive it in anyway?

Answer: Strictly speaking, yes. It seems to me that you inherited ownership of one-sixth of the house, but either your father had the right to live in it, or even if he didn't have the right, he did so anyway. Now that the house is being sold, if it is worth more than it was when your mother died, then you are making a capital gain. Being UK resident, you are liable to UK tax on your worldwide capital gains. If there is Spanish tax on this sale, most likely you will be eligible to double tax relief. As for not receiving any of the sale proceeds, I would imagine that you have a one-sixth share of the new apartment. Most likely this is an internal family matter that needs to be sorted out in a 'diplomatic' way.

234. Selling Part Of A Property's Garden

Question: I am considering selling a part of the garden of a house which I own and which is let and always has been. I bought the house for £350,000 and it is now worth £450,000. The part of garden to be sold is about one-third of the whole plot. I am expecting to sell the plot for £125,000. I would expect that the remaining house and garden would retain its value. As I see it, I would make a capital gain of £125,000 and would be liable for capital gains tax on the whole amount. An alternative view might be that when I bought the house the value of the house alone was say £200,000 and plot £150,000. This would mean that the one-third plot had a value of £50,000, so in this scenario my gain would be just £75,000. What is your view on my tax position?

Arthur Weller replies:
The (A / (A + B)) rule applies to your situation. See:
www.hmrc.gov.uk/manuals/cgmanual/CG12730+.htm and
www.hmrc.gov.uk/manuals/cgmanual/CG71800c.htm. You need to know how much you could sell the house and remaining land for, after having sold off this piece of land. Let's say this is £325,000 (£450,000 - £125,000). So (£125,000 / (£125,000 + £325,000)) = 27.7%. When 27.7% is applied to £350,000 the result is £97,222. This is therefore the base cost of this piece of land. So your gain is £125,000 - £97,222.

235. Any Tax If I Sell Land That Forms Part Of Garden?

Question: Is there tax to pay on the sale of land which forms part of the garden of the only residence if owners continue to live in the remaining part? If part of the income on the sale is then given to children as a gift, is that also free from tax, providing the parents survive the 7-year rule?

Answer: The capital gains tax exemption for a main residence includes grounds not exceeding half a hectare (approximately 1.25 acres), or such larger area as is appropriate to the size and character of the house.

If you sell some of the land, perhaps for building plots, the sale is covered by the exemption so long as the land was enjoyed as part of the garden and grounds and is sold either before the sale of the house, or at the same time as the sale of the house.

Gifting part or all of the proceeds of the sale to children is like any other gift (PET) as far as IHT is concerned. If the donor survives seven years, it falls out of the calculation of their IHT.

Inheritance Tax

236. What Is My Inheritance Tax Liability?

Question: If you inherit a property valued at £400,000 and which has an outstanding mortgage of £320,000. Are you still liable for IHT on values over £325,000 even though there is only capital of £80K in it?

Answer: Inheritance tax is due on the net value of the estate. So if the only two items attributable to the estate are a property valued at £400,000 and an outstanding mortgage of £320,000 then the net value of the estate is £80,000. Since this is below 2016-2017 £325,000 threshold there is no IHT.

237. At What Rate Do My Inheritors Pay Inheritance Tax?

Question: What is the rate for paying inheritance tax?

Answer: Inheritance tax is due at a rate of 40%

238. Inheritance Tax Planning - Which Is The Best Way?

Question: Whilst reading your December 2013 edition of the Property Tax Insider magazine, there is mention relating to inheritance tax planning and the fact that there are differences between whether a rental business generates investment property income or trading income. Can you please elaborate to what benefits each has and what can be done in the accounts to show that you are a majority of one and not the other?

Answer: If a rental business is classified as trading it should be eligible for business property relief from inheritance tax. It should also be eligible for rollover relief from capital gains tax for replacement of business assets. However, Class 2 and 4 National Insurance contributions must be paid on trading income. More important than what is shown in the accounts is the level of services provided with the accommodation. Letting furnished accommodation with extra services provided is investment income, whereas running a hotel is trading income. The distinction can sometimes be a narrow one.

239.   Is There A Tax Efficient Way To Make Gifts?

Question: What are the implications where parents make regular (monthly) financial gifts to their adult 'children' and is there a tax efficient way to make such gifts?

Answer: A gift from a parent to a child is a potentially exempt transfer (PET) as far as Inheritance Tax (IHT) is concerned. If the parent survives seven years after the gift, it will be disregarded as far as IHT is concerned.

However, if it is a regular small amount, it is likely to fall under the 'Normal expenditure out of income' rules, in which case it is exempt from IHT and is not a PET. To fall under these rules, the gift must be "part of your normal expenditure, and must not, taking one year with another, reduce your available net income (after all other transfers) below that required to maintain your usual standard of living".

The following may be possible: the parent could gift a proportion of a property to the child, e.g. 10% of a buy to let property that they are receiving rental income from. If the child is over 18, for tax purposes, it will be the child's income.

Since only 10% is being gifted, maybe there will not be any CGT on the transfer, because the gain is covered by the annual exemption. The income will be taxed on the child, instead of the parent, thus saving income tax.

240.   How Do I Minimise My Children's IHT On A Property?

Question: How do I minimise my children's inheritance tax on a property, whilst continuing to own that property during my lifetime?

Answer: It is not possible to avoid IHT on a residential property while continuing to own it. However:

a)   if it is commercial property used in the taxpayers business, it may qualify for Business Property Relief from IHT, and

b)   if not, it may be possible to put the property into a discretionary trust, which would take the property out of the estate of the taxpayer, while still allowing them a degree of control (i.e. as a trustee).

Consequently, if it is sold soon after death by the inheritor/recipient, there should be no CGT to pay because, presumably, it should be worth the same as it was when the original owner died. However, if it has gone up in value the inheritor/recipient will have made a capital gain. They will, of course, be able to use their capital gains tax annual exemption to reduce the amount on which they are liable to capital gains tax.

Just because it is your second property is not a reason for you to pay more/extra CGT or be the victim of another tax charge. However, you will not have the benefit of the principal private residence relief from capital gains tax of your first property (the property in which you live).

241. Can My Mother Live Rent-Free?

Question: My Mother is thinking of buying a retirement property which would be her main residence. She will sell the family home which she owns and presently occupies on her own.

My question is can my Mother give away the proceeds of the sale to her 3 children, and then live rent free in the retirement property which would be purchased and owned by 1 or more of her children. She has other assets in excess of the IHT threshold and has sufficient income to live on.

Answer: Your mother can certainly do so. The only question is what would be the taxation consequences? The gift to the 3 children would be a potentially exempt transfer (PET) as far as Inheritance Tax is concerned. Since the mother has given the sale proceeds to the child, who then goes and purchases property that the mother lives in, it would probably fall into the Pre-Owned Asset regime by virtue of Finance Act 2004 Chapter 15 paragraph 3.

The family should consider putting the property into trust, which has certain taxation advantages in this scenario. However, professional advice is essential to do this properly.

242. If I Die Will IHT Be Due Immediately?

Question: If have an estate worth £400,000. If I was to die tomorrow the estate would be passed to my children. Would they be liable to pay IHT immediately, which may mean that they have to sell the primary residence to pay the IHT bill?

Answer: If the deceased person's estate does not consist entirely of property then generally speaking IHT is due immediately. However, if the estate does consist of only property then it is possible to pay any IHT liability over a 10 year period.

243.   How Can I Avoid Inheritance Tax?

Question: How can I plan to avoid inheritance tax?

Answer: The single most cost-effective way to avoid IHT is to give away assets and hope to survive for seven years!

However, most people don't wish to do so for three reasons:

a)   they still want to benefit from the assets themselves,

b)   they don't trust the recipients, and

c)   a capital gain can often be triggered when gifting assets.

A discretionary trust can sometimes help to overcome b) and c).

Another effective way of avoiding IHT is to convert one's property into qualifying business assets which are 100% exempt from IHT. These are basically an interest in a trade (a sole trade or a partnership) or shares in a trading company that have been owned for two years. However, investments and shares in an investment company do not qualify.

A similar 100% exemption applies to qualifying agricultural property.

A not so commonly known method of avoidance is relevant to people with large amounts of regular annual income, some of which they don't use. If they get into the habit of giving away a proportion of their income every year while still maintaining their normal lifestyle, then even if they don't survive for seven years, this will fall out of their IHT computation.

244.   The Tax Implications of Selling Below Market Value?

Question: I am selling my house at under market value to my sister. My property is worth £190,000 on the open market but I am selling it to her for £100,000. Her mortgage company has said that I have to sign a Gift of Declaration for the £90,000. I have owned this property for 10 years and have lived in it up until July 2009 – it is the only property that I have ever owned and I have never rented it out.

Are there any tax implications for me before I exchange contracts?

Answer: The only tax implications for you on this transaction are that Inheritance Tax (IHT) is charged on a sale at undervalue i.e. the difference between the amount that you lose and the amount you receive in return, i.e. £190,000 - £100,000 = £90,000.

Since your 'gift' is to an individual you do not actually pay any IHT now (nor do you need to report this IHT matter to HMRC), and only if you die within 7 years will the £90,000 be included within your estate.

There is no Capital Gains Tax on the sale because of Principal Private Residence Relief. The period until Jul 09 is exempt due to actual occupation and the period after that is exempt due to the last three years' ownership rule.

245. Can I Offset A Loan From My Husband?

Question: My husband is prepared to loan me money for a buy-to-let property. Can I offset the interest of this loan from the rental income?

Answer: Yes, you can offset the interest of this loan from the rental income. However, since the loan is from a connected person, I would strongly advise you to draw up proper paperwork before the loan starts, showing a legitimate, authentic loan agreement. Also, ensure that the interest payments go from a bank account in your own name into a bank account in your husband's name, so that you can prove that the payments actually took place should the HMRC question you. (See pages IHTM28321-3 from the HMRC manuals, on the HMRC website.)

246. What Is The Tax Position For A Settlor And Trustee?

Question: Is it possible to create a property trust whereby the settlor adds a buy-to-let property to a trust and the property in the trust is not considered an asset of the settlor, but at the same time the settlor receives rental income from the trust? What are the tax implications for the settlor and for the trustees please?

Answer: The property in a discretionary Trust is not considered an asset of the settlor, for inheritance tax (IHT) purposes. If the settlor is also a beneficiary of the discretionary trust the trustees have a right, and the discretion, to pay the rental income to the settlor. However this arrangement is not so tax-efficient, because the trust income is taxed at 45% (the trust rate), and the assets within the trust are subject to the IHT exit charge and ten-year-charge rules.

247. Transferring Property From Sole To Joint Ownership - Any Pitfalls?

Question: I own my property, unencumbered, and it has a value of around £300,000. I am single and share my house with a friend of some 35 years standing and who is 18 years my junior. To protect his position I am keen to transfer my property to our joint names, but am concerned as to the cost of doing so in terms of tax and/or stamp duty. My estate today is about £750,000 and I would like to Will my share of the house to him. I am 71 and hope to be around for another seven years, and to protect my position would expect my friend to prepare a Will leaving his share to me should he predecease me. Apart from the costs referred to above, are there any other pitfalls that I should take into account?

Answer: Even though you mentioned 'I would Will my share', nevertheless from the rest of your question it is evident that you intend to make a lifetime gift of half your home to your partner. Since it is your main residence, there is no capital gains tax on the transfer. Since you are gifting for no consideration, there is no stamp duty land tax. With regard to Inheritance tax, if you continue to live in the house, it is a gift with reservation, and you will not have succeeded in taking £150,000 out of your estate, liable to IHT.

However if you look at page IHTM14332 (paragraph e)) of HMRC's inheritance tax manual, you can see that if your partner pays his share of the running costs while both of you live in the property at the same time, then it will not be a 'gift with reservation', and if you live for seven years after making the gift you will have succeeded in taking £150,000 out of your estate, saving £60,000 in IHT.

End of Guide

For more tax saving strategies please visit:

www.property-tax-portal.co.uk

To get better organised with our desktop based landlord software please visit:

www.propertyportfoliosoftware.co.uk

If you prefer landlord software that runs 'in the cloud' then visit our new brand:

www.landlordvision.co.uk

Lightning Source UK Ltd.
Milton Keynes UK
UKOW07f0556170416

272306UK00002B/2/P